Praise For…

Love Ever After
How My Husband Became My Spirit Guide

"Joy has a phenomenal story to tell. It's like *Conversations with God*…with an incredible love story! I couldn't put it down. This book lifted my heart and will create a healing for anyone who reads it."
— *Lisa Garr, "The Aware Show" KPFK*

"Your story is a great comfort for those who've suffered losses and provides great hope to carry on and build a new life at any age."
— *Nita Vallens,"Innervisions" KPFK*

"Meaningful and inspiring messages for understanding life both on earth and hereafter. The book is comforting, sound and inspirational. I would recommend it for anyone feeling a bit low and in need of uplifting practical cheer and guidance."
— *Whole Life Times*

"Filled with wisdom, warmth and wonder, this book is a page-turner. The love story is fascinating, but the questions and answers between Joy and her deceased husband Bob are truly a gift to the universe."
— *Joel Rothschild, author of "Signals"and "Hope"*

A Life and Death-Changing Book! Move over Sylvia Browne and James Van Praagh! Joy's story is amazing! I couldn't put it down. What a life! What an Afterlife!

Uplifting & Inspirational! Joy has written a book that gives everyone hope, especially concerning contacting loved ones who have crossed over. She also gives hope to those that feel abandoned and lost following the death of their mate. Thank you, Joy, for sharing your life with us!

Honest, Profound & Powerful! I read "Love Ever After" and was astounded by the tremendous information about life, death and the intent and organization of the Universe in such a concise and compelling form.

New Life Without Guilt! I lost my husband three years ago and Love Ever After gave me tremendous solace and inspiration. I can live and love again. It's amazing how Joy's deceased husband helped her find a new love in her life. I'm following Joy's instructions on how to contact my husband. If I can do this it'll mean more to me than anything in the world. Thanks for showing me that I can live my life without guilt.

A Real Page-Turner! A murder brought them together! But not even death could keep them apart! Sounds like Hollywood…but it's all true. Filled with wisdom and a real page-turner!

Realize Your Dreams! The 12-step program to manifesting your dreams absolutely works! When I declared out loud to Universe, "I am earning a good living as a writer," an offer came to freelance for a magazine the next day, and the offer since bloomed into a permanent position.

Simple and Easy to Use! Although I've read zillions of self-help books, they all seem to be saying the same thing. However, this book puts the most essential knowledge into the simplest and easiest-to-use form I've ever seen. The positive energy I found in this book gave me a much needed jolt that opened me up to possibilities that I could not see before. I plan to keep this book close at hand and I have been recommending it, and especially the 12-step program, to all my closest friends.

Life can change after reading a book! I never read anything more than once, and so far, I swear, I have read this book cover to cover twice!!! And I'm reading it chapter by chapter to my fiancée out loud! I was moved to visualize my life differently after finishing this book, and within two hours, the most wonderful opportunities were literally presented to me – FREE!!! ("In the past" I had financial issues) Thank you, Joy. You have helped me to make a serious and exciting change in my life!!!

Love Ever After

How My Husband Became
My Spirit Guide

. . . . . .

◆

Joy Mitchell Lisker

Love Ever After
How My Husband Became My Spirit Guide

ISBN: 978-0-9829322-0-9

More information:

DreaMaster Books
DreaMasterBooks@gmail.com
www.IJWeinstock.com

Layout & Design by EditWriteDesign.com
Original Graphic by aloha_17, iStockPhoto.com
Printed in the United States of America

For Bob, my beloved husband and mentor,
who encouraged me to pursue my dreams.
Thank you for all you have been and all
you continue to be in my life.

✦

Contents

✥ *This Life* ✥

✦

Part One

℘ 1 ℘

The Way We Were

"Breathe, Bob! Breathe!" I grabbed the plastic tube from the oxygen tank and inserted it in my husband's nose as he sat on the edge of the bed gasping for air. Then I dialed 911.

"They'll be here in a few minutes," I assured him, watching helplessly as he began to hyperventilate. "Slow down, honey. Try to take a deep breath."

I massaged his neck and shoulders and prayed for the paramedics to hurry. Waiting for them always felt like an eternity and I usually found myself holding my breath until they finally burst through the door.

My husband's emphysema had already resulted in 71 trips to the hospital emergency room in the last four years. It looked like this would be the 72nd. But as they wheeled him out on the gurney, I felt in my gut that this time was different. He usually winked at me or waved, or murmured something funny. That night his eyes were closed and he didn't utter a sound.

I sat down on the bed for a moment to get my bearings before throwing on some clothes and following the ambulance. I'd been through this so often, I knew there was no rush. The whole process of restoring his breathing to normal would take about two and a half hours. It always did.

I finished dressing, grabbed a book I'd been reading before

Bob's attack and walked out to the car. As I slid behind the wheel and started the engine, I began to feel a strange energy around me, as though I wasn't alone. At that moment I heard a voice saying, "I figured I could help you more from over here than from there." Instinctively, I turned to see if someone was in the back seat, but I was alone. I couldn't imagine what was going on. *Help me with what?* I wondered...but I was too exhausted to worry about it.

Arriving at the ER a few minutes later, Erica, the night nurse, greeted me from behind the glass partition as she had on every other visit for the last four years. But this time instead of asking me how I was doing or how I liked the book I was reading, she informed me that the doctor would be right with me.

I turned to cross the empty waiting room. Suddenly Dr. Franklin stood in front of me with a strange look on his face. My heart started to pound and my knees felt like rubber. He put his hand on my shoulder and told me as gently as he could that Bob had died in the ambulance on the way to the hospital. I fell forward and collapsed in his arms. The man who had been my friend for 36 years and my beloved husband for the last 11 was gone. And it felt as though my life was over, too.

The doctor gently led me to a chair. I sat there dazed, in complete denial. Finally he said, "If you'd like to see your husband, he's over there behind the curtain."

There were no other patients in the ER that night, which was unusual. I was totally alone as I made my way across the sterile white room to say goodbye to this incredible man. I took a deep breath before pulling aside the green curtain that surrounded his bed, but it didn't help much. I broke down and sobbed. And as I stood there, I wondered how I would ever live without him.

He didn't look much different physically, but it's a weird feeling to be with someone you love and realize that the life force has simply left and all you're looking at is an empty shell.

I thought to myself, "Oh my God! You're really gone!"

Instantly I heard him say, "No, I'm still here...but I'm freeeee!!" The words seemed to echo in my head.

I couldn't believe how happy he sounded, while I stood at his bedside feeling utterly devastated. The whole scene felt unreal, as though I was moving through some hideous nightmare and would wake up any minute. Then Bob's joy radiated around me in waves, and for a brief moment I saw him as a young man again.

Suddenly I understood what had happened in the car on my way to the hospital. Bob had already gone to the Other Side and had spoken to me! I still didn't know what he meant when he said, "I figured I could help you more from over here than from there." And I wouldn't for quite some time.

· · · · · ·

Although Bob left his body on July 24, 1995, his spirit is as much alive today as when he was here. The day he passed over, an entirely new kind of communication began between us—one which entirely changed my life and some of my beliefs about death.

Our new relationship feels different in many ways. Although we're not physically close, on a mental, emotional and spiritual level we're even more intimate than we were before. I was always honest with Bob, but now I can say anything and everything that's on my mind or in my heart. In fact, on numerous occasions I've ended up drenched in tears during our conversations, either from indescribable joy or an overwhelming feeling of awe.

It's ironic that during our life together, I was the one who introduced Bob to metaphysics and various spiritual concepts and now he's become my teacher, mentor and guide. He encouraged me to write our love story for two reasons: to let people know that relationships can and do continue after we leave our bodies, and to share the wisdom he's given me as I struggled to make a new life for myself.

· · · · · ·

Bob and I were an unlikely pair, to say the least. After being friends and confidants for 25 years, marriage was the furthest thing from our minds, mainly because we were opposites in almost every way. I was passionate about ballroom dancing — Bob had two left feet. I loved music — Bob couldn't carry a tune. I could play bridge all night — Bob was the poker type. And while I was born to shop — Bob would rather have had a root canal.

Bob was a conservative attorney, ex-marine and Kiwanis president. He loved betting on the horses, reading mystery novels, playing blackjack in Vegas, and collecting rare stamps. The man dressed in three-piece suits, for heaven's sake, and never owned a pair of jeans until we got married.

I, on the other hand, am an unconventional free spirit. As a professional astrologer, I often shock people with my radical ideas. Most of my friends see me as a cross between Doris Day and June Allyson, partly because I'm slender, blue-eyed, and blonde (with a little assistance), and partly because I'm usually happy and smile a lot. However, this innocent facade can be deceiving. On the inside, I'm as outrageous as Madonna and as radical as Shirley MacLaine. I'm fascinated with ideas that I call "progressive" and most people call "preposterous."

As a child, I loved Strauss waltzes, tap dancing, designing paper doll clothes, Shirley Temple movies, roller skating, anything chocolate, full skirts that twirled, and Sonja Henie, whose autographed picture adorned my dressing table throughout my teen years. While my introvert brother holed up in his room reading and writing, I was putting on shows in the backyard, writing and directing the sixth grade play, joining social and creative clubs, editing the high school annual and attending dances every weekend.

I grew up in Los Angeles in the days when it was safe for a 16 year-old girl to ride the streetcar home from downtown at 10 PM. My first job was at a drugstore cosmetics counter, but I had loftier ambitions. I planned to be a singer like my mother, who graduated from the Cincinnati Conservatory of Music and had a beautiful soprano voice. However, that changed at around 15 when my love of clothes and writing inspired me to fantasize about a career as an editor for a fashion magazine.

Almost nothing turned out the way I expected. I dreamed about graduating from college, launching a brilliant career, marrying my Prince Charming at around 25, having three children and living in a two-story colonial house with a winding staircase and picket fence. The reality wasn't even close. Eventually I lived in 28 houses—none of them two-story, much less colonial with a picket fence. I married three times and lost all three husbands. I had four children and lost two, one at a year old and the other at 12. And my only brother drowned at the age of 24.

What helped to prepare me for all those tragedies was the spiritual foundation my mother gave me. Unusually progressive for her generation, she was already involved in metaphysics by the time I was born, and in 1930 she became a Sunday School teacher at the fledgling Church of Religious Science in Los Angeles founded by Ernest Holmes. Metaphysics was a fairly new spiritual frontier at the time, and this church was a forerunner of what is now called the New Age movement.

I was never taught fear, guilt, prejudice and all the other dogma that was thrust on most of the kids I knew. Our ministers quoted from the Bible, the Torah, Buddha, Emerson, Confucius—anywhere they found the truth. When I was ten years old, I visited a Methodist church and was shocked to hear the minister claim that every other religion was wrong except his. Even then I knew there are many paths that lead to God, a concept that isn't nearly as revolutionary now as it was back in the 1930s. But to have been taught these beliefs as my spiritual roots was probably the greatest gift my mother gave me, and I am eternally grateful.

. . . . . .

Born in Philadelphia in 1926, Bob was a precocious child who taught himself to read at the age of three and worked his way through the entire family library by the time he was in the third grade. His adoring parents and two younger sisters considered him a genius.

When Bob was six, his father died of a heart attack and Bob became "the man of the house." His mother promptly moved the family to Hollywood, where she used the insurance money to buy a hat shop on the Sunset Strip.

Bob was only 16 when the Japanese bombed Pearl Harbor. Bored with his studies at Hollywood High, the idea of joining the Marines was suddenly all he could think about. A month after his 17th birthday he persuaded his mother to sign papers stating he was 18, and soon he was on his way to the South Pacific.

Bob loved being a Marine more than anything in the world. In fact, even though he was wounded, his adventures in WWII were probably the most treasured experiences of his life and the only part of his past Bob ever spoke of with nostalgia. He'd dredge up old war stories at the slightest provocation so he could relive the days when he was young and brave and living on the edge. When his ship caught fire off the coast of New Zealand, both of his legs were seriously burned and he had to endure painful skin grafts. But in spite of everything, he still loved being a Marine.

Returning to civilian life, Bob went to work for Technicolor studios in Hollywood, where he met and married Dorka, a film cutter, and started night school to become an attorney.

. . . . . .

The first time I met Bob Lisker I thought he was the most handsome man I'd ever seen. He barely noticed me. Not that it mattered. At 31 years old, I was madly in love with my second husband, Larry, and five months pregnant with our daughter. In fact, it was Larry who introduced me to Bob in the middle of a crowded Hollywood restaurant during "happy hour" in February 1959. Bob was 33, six feet tall, with a great body, dazzling smile and butch haircut, all of which made him a dead ringer for the movie star Dennis O'Keefe. Eventually we met his wife, Dorka, and the four of us began socializing.

Six years later, after Bob had become a successful attorney, one of his clients asked him to find a home for his pregnant daughter's baby. Bob jumped at the chance to become a father after 19 years of a childless marriage. However, Dorka was less than thrilled at the prospect of quitting a job she loved to raise a baby.

Whenever we visited them, the atmosphere was strained. Dorka was completely out of her element as a mother. In fact, she was a nervous wreck. Bob had suggested she go back to work and hire a nanny for the baby, whom they named Bruce, but she refused. It seemed as though she was determined to sacrifice her life for him. And in the end, she did.

In the early seventies, our two families drifted apart. Larry and I had our hands full running a small chain of record stores in the San Fernando Valley, as well as raising our daughter, Terri, and my son Elliot from my first marriage. I was also working as a professional astrologer and becoming fairly well known in the field.

Then in 1973, the marriage I thought was made in heaven began to disintegrate. On the surface, we seemed to have the perfect relationship, but there was one deadly flaw. Larry was the second alcoholic I'd chosen who, in spite of a handsome face and a charming facade, thoroughly hated himself and his life. And because he was so touchy about criticism, I stuffed every negative thought I had about him deep down inside until one morning I woke up and literally couldn't get out of bed. I was in agony. All the unspoken resentment and repressed rage of 15 years had finally paralyzed me.

After 11 doctors failed to find anything wrong with me, I knew that somehow I had to express my buried anger. And I knew that when I did, the marriage would be over. I'd waited far too long to come clean. Ultimately, it was my own self denial that destroyed the marriage…and almost destroyed me. When I finally expressed my feelings, it was too late to put the pieces back together. We divorced and the following year Larry died of cancer.

. . . . . .

Three years later I received a phone call out of the blue. "Hi stranger," Bob said in his deep, sexy voice. "I've been thinking about you guys and decided to track you down. How are you?"

When I told him about our divorce and Larry's death, he was shocked by the news and suggested we have lunch to catch up on our lives.

We met at Musso Frank's restaurant in Hollywood, in the front booth they had reserved for Bob every day for 15 years. And from that very first lunch, we began developing the friendship that would last a lifetime…and beyond.

We met for lunch or dinner about once a month and talked about our lives. Trading stories about our nameless clients, we realized that we were doing pretty much the same kind of work—he as an attorney and I as an astrologer were both counseling people.

Eventually I discovered that the only thing he and Dorka had in common was their adopted son, Bruce, whom Bob adored. They had stopped having sex entirely, which suited Dorka just fine, since that was never her idea of a good time. However, there were plenty of other women who were only too happy to fill Bob's sexual needs. Some were clients who were divorcing their husbands and others were the ex-wives of his male clients. Since they were right there in his lap, so to speak, it was hard to resist the temptation...and he usually didn't.

I used to call Bob my Rock of Gibraltar, because he was the only man I knew who could remotely be considered stable. In contrast to all the creative artists, musicians, writers and unemployed geniuses I seemed to attract, Bob was the one person who was always there for me. He was generous, appreciative, encouraging and fun to be with. Bob was also a scrupulously honest attorney. I admired his business ethics and so did his clients because he always got the job done as quickly and economically as possible. And if some of his elderly clients couldn't get to his office, he went to them. I received dozens of touching letters from these people when he died. After all, they had lost their Rock of Gibraltar, too.

But as much as I liked and respected Bob, I wasn't really in love with him in those days. I seemed to be attracted to men who needed fixing. And Bob didn't fit that pattern at all. At least not then.

However, there was another reason I didn't allow myself to fall in love. I knew Bob would never leave Dorka, no matter how miserable he was. He was far too responsible for that—and far too much a creature of habit. He may not have been sexually faithful, but Bob was endlessly loyal. He used the same barber shop, Chinese laundry, insurance company, stock broker and accountant for over 35 years.

He hated change and usually managed to avoid it at all costs. As far as his marriage was concerned, I knew he'd stick it out, in spite of everything, until one of them died.

· · · · · ·

On March 10, 1983 I received a phone call that instantly changed the lives of four people—Bob, Dorka, Bruce and me.

"Dorka has been beaten and stabbed." I'd never heard Bob sound so shaken. "She's on the operating table now."

I gasped. "Oh my God! Where are you?"

"Valley Hospital," he replied.

"Who did it?"

There was a long pause before he answered. "The police think Bruce did it. But he's denying it."

I was so stunned, I barely managed to stammer, "Whhh…..where is he now?"

"In jail. He said he got to the house and found Dorka lying in the hallway bleeding and unconscious, so he called 911 and then me. When I got there the paramedics were putting her in the ambulance, and Bruce was handcuffed in the back of the police car."

I could hardly digest what he was saying. "Oh, Bob! I'm so sorry."

"Gotta go now. I'll call you later." His voice was flat, without inflection, yet full of desperation.

Dorka died on the operating table a few hours later without ever regaining consciousness. And the truth died with her.

౩ 2 ౬

Happily Ever After

I didn't see Bob for almost a month after Dorka's funeral, but when we talked on the phone it was obvious that he was barely able to function. He was completely overwhelmed by his daily visits to Bruce, who was still in jail awaiting trial for murder. On top of that, his frequent consultations with the police and the public defender made it difficult for him to keep up with his busy law practice.

The stress was causing him to smoke even more than usual and, as a result, he was developing severe breathing problems. As far as his personal life was concerned, he'd withdrawn into a shell, refusing dinner invitations and offers of moral support from everyone he knew.

Despite failing a lie detector test, Bruce steadfastly maintained his innocence. He insisted that he had arrived at the house and found his mother unconscious on the floor. Bob wanted desperately to believe his son.

For years, he'd come home almost every night to referee fights between Bruce and Dorka, but he refused to acknowledge the seriousness of the situation. When Dorka begged him to do something, Bob argued that Bruce was just being rebellious, like all kids his age.

At 16, Bruce had already been expelled from three schools, treated by half a dozen psychologists and spent 18 months at a camp for problem boys in Northern California. When he returned, Bob set him up in an apartment nearby where he soon gravitated to a group of addicts whose primary goal each day was scoring drugs. Small for his age and with little self-esteem, lying and stealing became a way of life.

As pragmatic and down-to-earth as Bob was, when it came to his son he was in total denial. He buried his head in the sand, blindly accepting Bruce's lies and alibis because he loved him so much. Now he blamed himself for ignoring the problem.

· · · · · ·

By the 4th of July weekend of 1983, after four months of seclusion, I hoped that Bob might be ready to venture out into the world. My daughter, Terri, was now the lead singer in a rock band, so I invited him to her concert at the Universal Amphitheater in Los Angeles.

Bob had never been to a rock concert before, so when he accepted my invitation, I figured he was just being polite. However, to my surprise, by the second song he was on his feet with the rest of the crowd, moving and clapping to the music. He loved it!

The following month Bob invited me to his home for a barbecue by the pool, and I immediately sensed a different energy between us. As we sat on the patio talking, I met his gaze over my glass of wine and saw the sparkle return to his eyes. Then he reached for my hand and I was surprised to feel a sexual connection I'd never experienced with him before. He was obviously getting ready to come out of isolation! Finally, on that hot August night, we unleashed all the passion that had been hiding under a beautiful friendship for over 25 years. And that was the beginning of a whole new chapter in both of our lives.

As our relationship blossomed and became more physically and emotionally intimate, Bob started to soften and let down his guard. By Christmas, I realized I'd fallen in love with my best friend, my hero and my Rock of Gibraltar. Here was the one person I could always count on, and now at last he needed me to support him through the enormous emotional trauma of coping with Dorka's murder, Bruce's imprisonment and the trial.

Bob also drew strength from the love and support of my children, who were probably the greatest gifts I ever gave him. He adored them both and encouraged them in every way possible. In return, they loved and respected him more than any man they'd ever known.

My son, Elliot, was playing keyboards with a local band at the time and Bob loved to go the clubs where they performed. I'd watch in amazement as this guy with two left feet when it came to ballroom dancing, would get out on the floor and rock and roll like a teenager. Elliot had been an outstanding gymnast and straight A-student in high school and had shone so brightly that part of him wanted to stay a kid forever. But Bob became a powerful role model and encouraged him to focus his extraordinary talent into a successful career as a composer and recording engineer.

Terri was the sunshine of Bob's life. For her, Bob was the model of what a really great father and husband could be. Intelligent, sensitive, caring and devoted to her family, Terri began a successful acting career at the age of 15, appearing on TV and in movies, but her greatest passion was music. So after turning down more than a dozen TV series for fear of getting stuck in a lengthy contract, she finally walked away from acting to follow her musical dreams. In the years that followed, Bob was so proud of her success, he made sure we attended as many of her concerts as possible.

In the spring of 1984 Bob and I moved into a beautiful condo in the Valley and were married later that year.

· · · · · ·

As Bob's wife, I was finally permitted to accompany him on his weekly visits to Bruce at the Juvenile Detention Facility in downtown Los Angeles. I soon began to see how traumatic this experience was for Bob, especially since he believed Bruce was innocent. I tried to imagine how I'd feel if one of my own kids had been locked away for murder. Just the thought of it was horrifying!

Naturally, the murder and all its gory details were the subject of constant discussion between us as we tried to piece together the truth of what actually happened. We'd consider every possible scenario for hours at a time, but kept coming up empty-handed.

Bruce convinced Bob that Dorka's murderer was an 18-year-old drug addict and convicted felon named John Ryan, one of Bruce's drug buddies. The night before the murder Dorka told Bob that John had come to the house that day to ask for work, saying he needed money to visit his sister in San Francisco. Dorka fixed him lunch, but told him she had no jobs for him.

Bruce claimed that on the morning of the murder, he drove to his parents' house to borrow some tools to fix his car. He rang the doorbell and no one answered. Seeing Dorka's car in the garage, he figured she must be home. So he went around to the back patio, peered through the sliding glass door and saw her lying on the floor of the entry hall. He removed the glass louvers from the kitchen window, climbed in and found his mother unconscious with three knives in her back and a rope around her neck. Although bleeding profusely, she was still breathing. He removed the knives, dialed 911 for help, then called his dad.

When Bob arrived, the house was a wreck—blood was

splattered all over the floor and walls and most of the furniture was overturned. Dorka had obviously been chased through several rooms and bludgeoned with Bruce's baseball trophy and his exercise bar before being stabbed and choked.

As controlled as Bob was, I could see that his visits to Bruce were affecting him more all the time. His health began to reflect his turbulent emotional state and the terrible guilt he carried for not having confronted the situation with Bruce years earlier. He was seeing a therapist twice a week and I was giving him all the support, understanding and strength I could.

Bruce's trial finally took place in December 1985, two years and nine months after the murder. Considering his history of drug addiction, expulsion from three schools and his miserable relationship with Dorka, not to mention his presence at the scene of the crime, it didn't take the jury long to pronounce him guilty. He was convicted of second degree manslaughter and sentenced to 15 years-to-life. Since we both wanted desperately to believe Bruce was innocent and would be acquitted, the long, painful trial ended with me sobbing hysterically in the courtroom and Bob biting his lips to hold back the tears.

. . . . . .

Bob needed to know the truth about Dorka's murder and often said he wished there were some way he could talk to her. I knew that other people had made contact with loved ones on the Other Side through various meditation techniques, so I suggested he try meditating and ask to speak with her. But he was so rooted in his own black and white concepts of reality that I didn't think he believed it was possible. He was always tolerant of my explorations into astrology and spirituality, but I'm sure he never expected to get involved himself.

One evening I called him to dinner, and when he didn't answer, I went into our bedroom and found him lying on the bed. At first I thought he was taking a nap, until suddenly he opened his eyes and said, "Guess who I've been talking to?"

I shrugged.

"Dorka!" he replied. "You told me all I needed to do was meditate and ask for her. So I did and she started talking to me!"

I must admit, I was as astounded as Bob was. I could hardly believe that my conservative, ex-marine husband was talking to someone on the Other Side! But he was such a skeptic, I knew he wouldn't lie about that sort of thing.

"Now I'm going to find out who killed her," he announced.

I waited and watched as he silently communicated with Dorka, hoping she'd say something, anything, that would finally give him some peace of mind and alleviate his feelings of guilt. Tortured by this tragic situation, he was desperate to find some answers.

Finally, he opened his eyes and I could see the disappointment in them.

"What did she say?" I asked

"She can't tell me. She says there are some things we're not supposed to know, but someday—when it makes no difference to us—we'll learn the truth."

At the time, neither of us understood what that meant. It only became clear many years later.

ഔ 3 ର

New Dimensions

Though he was born Jewish, Bob had little or no interest in religion or spirituality before we started dating. However, after we got married, I noticed that some of my unconventional ideas were starting to rub off on him.

On October 2, 1985, a few weeks after his "conversation" with Dorka, Bob said he'd like to connect with a spirit guide. I could hardly believe my ears! Was this the same practical, down-to-earth man I'd known for 25 years? The one who never believed in anything he couldn't experience with one of his five senses? There was obviously more going on beneath those conservative three-piece suits than I'd realized!

Bob had heard me talk about spirit guides who, like guardian angels, we can turn to for guidance. Suddenly he was curious about them. I suggested using hypnotism, which I'd been studying for many years. But since Bob usually liked to stay in control, I wasn't sure if he could relax enough to get into a receptive hypnotic state. I also assumed it would take several sessions before we got any results.

Anxious to get started, Bob stretched out on the sofa in the den, closed his eyes, and I proceeded to hypnotize him. First I helped him let go of his physical and mental tension, then invited his spirit guides to communicate with us. Frankly, I wasn't expecting much on our first attempt, so I was absolutely amazed at what happened next.

Bob's guide came through almost immediately and introduced himself as *Yallen*. It was obvious that Bob had made a connection with something or someone outside his own consciousness. Not only did Yallen's deep monotone voice and authoritarian manner sound decidedly different from Bob's, but the information he imparted could not have come from my conventional husband. I'll never forget the excitement I felt when Yallen first spoke.

Immediately I began asking questions. What follows is an excerpt from our first taped session.

Can you tell me anything about yourself, Yallen? Where you are? Whether you're male or female?

> **I am in the Universe, but I cannot describe where I am because you would not understand. I have been both sexes in various lives as well as a non-sexed creature and I have had several earth experiences. My experience now is to be a communicator, which is like a teacher, but only to the extent of exposing the facts. It may well be that if Bob decides to continue, I will be replaced by another teacher for more direct and specific communication. Bob is not my only communicant. There are several other humans learning from me as well.**

At this point I felt like I'd hit the supernatural jackpot. Now I could finally get the answers to the questions I'd been asking all my life. But I knew I had to restrain myself and focus on the real reason for this contact: to find out the truth about Dorka's murder.

Will you give me any information on people I know who have passed over?

No, that is not my function. I am here to communicate and educate only—to broaden your comprehension. At this time I am not a being to be contacted for information, although my communicant at some point may reach a new level where a different being is assigned to that experience.

Damn! I was so disappointed that we wouldn't be able to find out anything about Dorka, and I knew Bob would be, too. Then it occurred to me how bizarre it was that although Bob had never shown any interest in the occult, he was the one who had made contact with a spirit guide.

Will Bob be asking you his own questions one of these days?

Yes, he will learn. And eventually he will be able to do all of this without hypnosis simply by switching on and switching off. He is not yet ready for that because he is too self-centered and too concerned about his immediate problems. This is still a bit of a toy or a game to him, when in fact, it is the reality of universal creation. He cannot yet comprehend that, but he will do so or there will be a different direction for his future experience. I cannot tell what will happen because it is something he must decide and follow his own course, whatever that may be.

Our conversation continued for over half an hour, and I was so thrilled I could hardly contain myself. Not only did Yallen provide fascinating information on a variety of metaphysical subjects, but this was definitely the most unusual experience I'd ever shared with Bob, and it made me look at this man I thought I knew so well in an entirely different light.

As I slowly brought him out of his trance, I couldn't wait to discuss what had just happened. He had barely opened his eyes when I started questioning him. "Do you realize what you just did, honey? My God, how did you feel? Are you exhausted?"

Bob stretched his neck and rotated his shoulders a few times as he attempted to refocus his consciousness. "No, I feel fine. You know, I was surprised at how easy it was."

He was surprised? I was flabbergasted! "Me too," was all I managed to say.

"How did it sound?" he asked, still in a slight stupor.

"Surprisingly different," I said, "like someone else." I leaned over and began rubbing his neck and shoulders. "Did you actually hear what was said?"

He nodded. "Some of it."

"Do you want to do it again sometime?" I asked.

"Why not? Maybe I can get some answers about Bruce." Which was exactly the answer I expected.

·   ·   ·   ·   ·

So that was the beginning of our extraordinary adventure with Bob's spirit guides, which continued off and on for the next ten years. These conversations opened up a fascinating new dimension to our relationship. After a while, Bob didn't need to be hypnotized—he just closed his eyes and Yallen would start talking. Eventually he didn't even have to close his eyes to make the connection. Since it was pretty easy for me to distinguish Bob's voice from Yallen's, sometimes we'd carry on a three-way conversation over dinner.

Although Bob had access to the answers through Yallen, I

seemed to have most of the questions. What fueled Bob's interest was the possibility of getting information about the murder. And although we received a great deal of helpful guidance, much to Bob's disappointment we were never given a definitive answer regarding Bruce's guilt or innocence.

One day Bob told me Yallen was gone and someone else was talking to him who called himself the *Director*. We were both a little surprised until we remembered what Yallen had said the night of our first conversation—as we progressed in knowledge and reached a new level of comprehension, a different spirit guide might take his place.

The Director made it very clear that he was not there to solve other people's problems or make predictions, but he helped immeasurably with Bob's health issues. For example, when Bob was having trouble breathing, sometimes I'd ask the Director if his condition was serious enough to call the paramedics, or we'd ask if a new medication was right for Bob. He always gave us accurate advice and eventually we came to value his counsel even more than Bob's doctors, since he knew Bob better than anyone.

Once in a while Bob would sit at the computer and use two fingers to type out what he was hearing in his head from the Director. These are the first words Bob transcribed.

When you sought to reach your late wife, a rare jump occurred in your ability to communicate. In almost an instant, you became a conduit to the Universal Spirits. I am the Director. I am not any different from your other teacher, but I have greater awareness of the workings of the universe and the authority to give much of this knowledge to you.

You managed to contact Dorka and your guide very

quickly, which others beside yourself have accomplished without understanding how or why. Still other human beings, in spite of continual effort, have never learned how to make contact.

For whatever reason, you were given an opportunity sought by many to receive information that is not generally available to physical beings. Yet nothing in your prior, rather prosaic, life would indicate this, other than the violent series of events regarding your wife that gave rise to your efforts to make contact. You were selected because these events caused you, a skeptic, or at least a relatively stable, conservative type, to break through to your own subconscious mind and relate to the spiritual world.

As you already know, I communicate with you by placing thoughts in your mind. I give you these words to report, knowing that you will do so as accurately as possible, without amplification or editorializing. It is time for all physical beings to be made aware of the greater existence from which they come and to which they will return. The learning may frighten some, may encourage others. It may be perverted or disbelieved by many. Regardless, the lessons shall be made available to all to use or not use as they see fit.

As a result of your occasional receptiveness, you have made some progress. Oh, I'm not criticizing, simply commenting. We recognize that each of us proceeds at our own pace to learn the lessons and have the experiences that are ours to receive during our physical lives.

Bob knew that a wealth of information was available, but

was never willing to spend the time required to produce a book, which the Director wanted him to write. He was much more interested in playing tennis, going to the race track, or gambling in Las Vegas.

· · · · · ·

In 1987 Bruce was transferred to San Quentin prison near San Francisco and we traveled there to see him every other month for three years. Understandably, these weekends were a horrendous emotional drain on Bob, who was already burdened with unbearable grief and guilt. Seeing the son he loved locked up in prison broke his heart all over again each time we visited. In the meantime, Bob was employing every legal maneuver he could think of to overturn the verdict, but so far nothing was working.

According to the principles of metaphysics, there is a significant relationship between our illnesses and our emotional well being. For example, problems with the throat often indicate that someone is having trouble "swallowing" a truth or is withholding something that needs to be expressed. I suspected that part of Bob's breathing problem was emotional—he was trying to hold his breath until Bruce got out of prison.

As a smoker myself, I'd learned that cigarettes create a smokescreen I could hide behind to keep from exposing my real feelings. So although the emphysema that was destroying his lungs was the result of 50 years of heavy smoking, the cigarettes also served to mask the grief that was breaking his heart. This vicious cycle would eventually halt the breathing process and end his life.

When I married Bob I thought I'd finally overcome my attraction to addicts. From the time I was in high school I'd made a career out of fixing broken people—and I always managed to find plenty of them. My first two husbands were alcoholics, one boyfriend was a pothead and another was addicted to gambling. On top of that, all the men in my life smoked. But then, so did I. No big deal, I thought. How little I knew!

Bob had stopped drinking before we were married at the insistence of his doctor, but cigarettes were another matter entirely. His whole existence seemed to depend on them. When Bob was diagnosed with emphysema, *I* was the one who stopped smoking! Bob told me he'd quit, but in reality he'd just found more resourceful ways to secretly continue smoking.

On one of our visits to Bruce, we had to call the paramedics from our hotel room in Sacramento because Bob couldn't breathe. After they left with Bob, I found cigarettes in the pocket of his jacket and I was livid! I drove to the hospital, stormed into the intensive care unit and screamed at my poor husband, lying there helpless with half a dozen tubes coming out of him. They finally had to send in a social worker to calm me down. Bob was mortified, but he promised never to smoke again. And this time he really meant it.

Yeah, right! That was a year and a half before he died. And even though I couldn't figure out why he was still coughing so much, I guess I just wanted to believe him.

About a week after Bob's death the custodian of our condominium showed me where Bob stashed his cigarettes in the lobby of our building. I was stunned. The addiction that originally seemed so harmless—and was the same as my own— is the one that killed him. And I finally realized that my own greatest addiction was not to cigarettes. I was addicted to addicts!

· · · · · ·

I was brushing my teeth the morning after Bob died when he started talking to me again.

"Get rid of the oxygen tank and the breathing machine," he

said. At first I was startled. Then I looked over at the corner of the room where the five-foot oxygen tank had stood for the last four years, covered with the pale blue skirt I'd made to hide its ugly chipped green paint. In its place, I visualized a beautiful, tall, green plant—which, incidentally, materialized early the next morning in the form of an eight foot palm sent by two of my dearest friends.

"Throw out all my prescriptions on the bathroom sink and everything else in sight that's connected with my illness," Bob instructed. "You can go through the cupboards and drawers later and toss out the rest of the medications. I want you to fill this house with love and beauty."

I went over to the bed and sat down, awash in tears that seemed endless. At the same time, I felt completely surrounded and protected by Bob's loving energy.

He kept repeating "Fill your life with love and beauty. Let this house express who you are. You can create your own paradise right here."

But how could I possibly stay here alone in this home that we had created together? It would just keep reminding me of a life that no longer existed. Part of me wanted to run away from my grief and loss to somewhere that wouldn't keep forcing me to remember. At the same time, I was terrified of severing my precious connection to this man who had been the love of my life.

Of course, I had no idea then that he would always be near me. I sat there for a long time in a state of total confusion about all the decisions ahead of me. I hadn't the slightest idea how I was going to get through this, but I could hear his voice deep inside me saying, "Don't worry, I'm with you. Just take one step at a time."

That night I fell into bed, exhausted from the emotional

demands of making phone calls and planning the memorial service. Curling up on my right side, I was just starting to drift off, when suddenly I felt Bob's presence in bed with me. Then I actually felt his hand on my back. This seemed strange, yet somehow comforting at the same time. Slowly his hand moved down to caress my body. And that's when I started getting uncomfortable. I knew I was awake—this was definitely not a dream. So what was going on here? Maybe I was just imagining the whole thing. I squirmed around and readjusted my position. The next thing I knew, I felt his hand between my legs. I moved around again, hoping to shake off the feeling. When he started caressing my breasts, I decided I must really be losing it. I soon realized that this was supposed to be foreplay. He was trying to warm me up. Oh my God, I thought, he wants to have sex with me!

At this point I freaked out. When I finally calmed down, I spoke to him directly.

"Bob, I love you dearly, but this is just too weird. You have to stop this. I can't handle it."

He stopped immediately, thank God, and never tried again. I mean, I could handle talking to a spirit, but having sex with one was just too much, even for me. I felt badly for a moment, afraid I'd hurt his feelings. But I sensed no disappointment on his part, or that his ego was involved in any way.

Since then, I've learned that spirits often hang around for awhile after leaving their bodies, because their personalities are still closely connected to the earth plane and their loved ones. That's why it's easiest to communicate with someone for the first few days after crossing over. So many people are focusing their attention on them that the collective energy usually keeps them here until after the funeral or memorial service.

Bob's service was a magnificent celebration of his life. More than 200 people crowded into the little Religious Science Church to hear his relatives and friends share their love for this amazing man.

When Terri sang "The Wind Beneath My Wings" accompanied by Elliot on the piano, the song gave us all permission to let the tears flow. Then Elliot choked back his own tears to relate a story I'd never heard before. When he was six years old and met Bob for the first time, he thought to himself, "I wish he was *my* dad." He'd never gotten along well with his stepfather, but he instantly recognized the kind of dad he wanted. Eventually he got his wish.

But the person everyone else was honoring that day—the brilliant, conservative, respected businessman—was only a part of who Bob really was. As his favorite song, "The Marines' Hymn," concluded the service, I could feel his spirit around me like a warm caress and he was smiling. I felt the joy of his newfound freedom and his utter relief at being released from the body that had become his prison. And because we had shared so many years of communication with his guides, I also knew that he wasn't gone.

Joy Mitchell Lisker

❧ The Afterlife ❧

✦

Part Two

℘ 4 ☙

How I Talk to Bob

Bob told me more than once that we'd be writing a book together someday. Frankly, I never believed him because he was a terrible writer. He was fine with letters and legal documents, but that's about it. He loved to read and was convinced he could write a mystery novel as well as Robert Ludlum, his favorite author. It was just a case of putting his mind to it, he said. So one day he actually sat down and wrote about a dozen pages. They were dreadful! That's why I could never imagine what in the world he was talking about...until now.

· · · · · ·

When Bob and I first began communicating, we just talked about trivial things while I was taking a shower, putting on make-up or driving the car. But finally, we started having conversations every morning as part of my regular meditation.

According to Bob, it's not difficult to connect with someone when love is present on both sides, since emotions are the bridge between dimensions. In other words, feelings are the glue that binds us together, whether in the physical or the spiritual dimension. Therefore, the same feelings that connect us here in physical form continue to unite us to those on the Other Side.

I usually meditate in the morning before my conscious mind

gets busy with mundane affairs. Sitting in a comfortable chair in my breakfast room near a large window with an expansive view of trees, mountains, sky and clouds, I start by taking deep breaths and completely relaxing my whole body. I find it most effective to breathe in through my nose and out through my mouth. Then I unfocus my gaze and, with my eyes open, stare at the top of a mountain ridge across the valley.

After a few minutes, I begin to see an aura of light emanating from the top of the ridge and I invite Bob to join me. (It's important that you ask for the spirit by name). Then I either ask a question or mention a topic I want to talk about. But I can also meditate by staring at a crack in the ceiling, a light fixture or the leaf of a tree. It doesn't really matter what I stare at as long as I keep my eyes unfocused. So whether you gaze out of a window or simply stare at a wall, choose a space that feels comfortable and serene.

Sometimes I meditate with my eyes closed, but I've found that it's usually harder to clear my mind that way. Some people just close their eyes and are able to cancel out their thoughts quite easily, but this isn't the case for me. When I close my eyes I may not be distracted by seeing what's around me, but the lack of visual stimulation allows my thoughts to take over and run rampant. So my mind just keeps busy resisting and rejecting all those thoughts. Somehow the process feels backwards. So I focus my attention *first* and then all the extraneous thoughts just naturally fall away.

Repeating mantras, prayers or any simple phrase works well for many people. However, this technique becomes so intense for me that it often shuts out Bob. By unfocusing my eyes and staring at something, either indoors or outdoors, my mind seems to clear automatically...sort of like daydreaming. This takes a little practice, of course, but there's nothing difficult about it.

At a certain point I let go of my own thoughts and *listen*. After a few minutes, I usually start hearing words and ideas in my head, but I don't hear a human voice. Rather, thoughts come through my mind that don't feel like mine and the element of surprise is always present. I never know what's coming next and I don't try to guess. I stay in the moment.

Sometimes an entire concept bursts into my mind all at once and I feel I've suddenly understood a complex idea in a split second. It's like an "Ah-ha!" Then I have to take it apart and put it into words so I can share it. Bob explains this in a later chapter when he describes how he learns and communicates on the Other Side. He calls it a "living informational unit." Lots of channelers get these "globs" of information.

Obviously, my spiritual background was an important factor in creating the foundation for this experience with Bob. By the time he died, I had already communicated with several friends and family members who had passed over. However, I had never developed an ongoing relationship with any of them. But the fact that I already trusted the process was an enormous help in opening me to receive Bob's messages. Without personal experience, you can't really *know* that this kind of connection is possible, but your *belief* in the possibility will go a long way in allowing it to happen.

After talking with Bob for a few weeks, I began feeling the urge to pick up a pen. The minute I did, the words came spilling into my mind faster than I could write them down. In fact, as I took his dictation, I was extremely grateful for my knowledge of shorthand. Sometimes when I first pick up the pen, nothing comes through at all. So I just start writing something like "Hi Bob. How are you today? I'm feeling pretty good, had a fabulous time last night," and so forth. I find that this primes the pump, so to speak. Then I write down a specific question about my life, or a philosophical question about life in general, and pretty soon I start "hearing" an answer. Then I'm off and running.

Bob never tells me *what* to ask, since that has to come from my own interests. However, if I never ask for anything, he can't help me much. I'm like the "plug" and he's the wall socket. I'm the one who makes the connection that creates the electricity or juice. Bob and the other guides who have come through since Bob left his body, are like sets of encyclopedias that contain all the knowledge in the Universe. The answers are always there, but if I never ask any questions, all their wisdom doesn't do me much good.

And now, dear reader, I hope you will be as fascinated and inspired by my conversations with Bob as I have been. In the following pages I am honored and delighted to share his love and wisdom with you.

৫০ 5 ৫৪

What Happens When We Die

About three weeks after Bob passed on, I felt a strong compulsion to pick up a pen and record some of the fascinating conversations we were having. The instant I did, an overwhelming sense of relief washed over me, as if that's exactly what Bob had been waiting for. I knew immediately I was on the right track. This is what I wrote that day.

August 17, 1995

Good morning, my love. I miss you like crazy and I'm trying so hard to keep it together. Why did you leave me?

> **I miss you, too, sweetheart. I left because there was really nothing more I needed to do. Just going to work every day wasn't enough to fulfill me any more. Besides, with all my health problems, my sex life was pretty much over—as you well know—and I was getting discouraged in my efforts to get Bruce out of prison. On the other hand, I was terrified about how to handle things when he did get out.**

My pride was too much involved in that situation, I'm afraid. I was always so worried about what people would think. Of course, from where I am now I can see what a waste of time that is! Almost every soul who crosses over recognizes this and wishes they hadn't spent so much time and energy worrying about what others think.

I was also tired of lugging around that breathing machine everywhere I went and being rushed to the hospital all the time. It was getting to be a real drag, and I was afraid that eventually my body would become even more of a burden—to both of us. That's why I left, my love—and yet, I never really left, you know.

Yes, I notice, but I still don't like being without your physical body.

I understand. But things were pretty much in order by this summer. The kids were finally married and settled down and I'd tied up a lot of loose ends.

You certainly did. I found out that in the last three days you called both your sisters just to say hello, which you hardly ever did. And then you took your secretary to lunch, which you hardly ever did except on her birthday.

My spirit already knew I was preparing to go, but my conscious mind wasn't aware yet.

So are you saying that we actually have a choice about whether to stay or go?

Absolutely. The choice is either made beforehand, by consciously or unconsciously wishing for the life to end, or at the point of death.

Well, what actually happened when you died?

At first I couldn't breathe and then I just decided to let go. When I did, there was kind of a *whoooosh* sound as I moved through something like a tunnel. And yes, there was light at the end of the tunnel.

I felt kind of strange asking the next question, but I plunged ahead anyway.

What did it feel like to die?

A little bit like falling asleep and waking up light and free and surrounded by love. You know how it feels when you have those dreams where you're flying and dancing in the air without any weight? Well, it's sort of like that—a state of pure love that's hard to experience as long as you're in a body.

I must say, it's kind of a shock to find yourself still functioning after leaving your body, but that's what happens. My mind was immediately in what you would consider an altered state, and my perception was entirely different.

What do you mean?

Humans experience similar states on mind altering drugs, through meditation, hypnosis, devotional states of ecstasy and what you call psychic experiences.

Weren't you afraid?

No. Once I made the decision, I wasn't afraid. That's why it happened so fast. Most people keep resisting because they think death is the end. They don't believe there's anything else after this life, so they hold on much too long and suffer needless pain and agony.

When that happens, the process always feels longer. Not that it is, it just feels that way. You experience the same kind of thing where you are. When you're doing something you love, time always seems to go faster than when you're doing something you hate, like sitting in a dentist's chair or waiting in line.

After you died, did you look down and see your body?

Yes, for a moment. It looked like a worn out suit. And that's when I finally understood what I'd learned earlier from my own spirit guides: we are not our bodies, we are immortal spirits.

Were you aware of my coming to the hospital to see you?

Of course. It's not like I suddenly went off somewhere into the sky, you know. It's not like that. I didn't go anywhere, except out of my body. So of course I was hanging around, especially the first few days. That's why you felt me so strongly in the beginning. I had no regrets about leaving, but my love for you and the kids kept me connected—or earthbound—for awhile.

I certainly knew you were around when you were trying to make love to me that first week. Now you must admit, honey, that was pretty bizarre.

I'm sorry, but I couldn't resist. I wasn't sure how you would react, but you were so beautiful, and so sad. I just wanted to love you.

Well, it was a bit more than I could handle at the time, but I hope I didn't hurt your feelings.

No. My feelings and reactions in this state aren't the same as yours. That's because now I have an instant understanding of the intentions behind your actions. I stopped as soon as I realized you were getting spooked. I'm sorry about that.

So how much are you aware of me now? Do you actually see me and what I'm doing?

I don't "see" as you do, but my perception includes things *you* can't see normally. I perceive the energy around you and inside you. I perceive you more as energy than matter, and you know what I mean by that because you've seen that energy, too. You're not solid, you know. Your body is constantly moving and vibrating. In fact, that's how your body is continually being formed and reformed.

You remember that old saying, "If you keep looking cross eyed you'll stay that way"? Well, that's actually true on a slower scale of evolvement. The more you frown or cry or smile or feel happy or excited—that's how your body is formed. In fact, the reason you still look so young is because you're happy.

You mean there are physical rewards for being happy?

Of course. There are consequences for everything you do and think and feel. That's part of what I'm learning about now.

Can you tell me where you are? Or is there a "where?" I know it's a different reality, but can you give me a description of some kind that I can understand?

You're right—there is no "where." Actually, I'm "everywhere." And since there is no time, I am everywhere at the same time. Your question is kind of like asking where the air is on your planet. It's everywhere.

When Jesus said, "In my house there are many mansions," he meant "many dimensions." And these dimensions all exist in the same general space. Since everything in the Universe is a form of energy, each dimension operates within its own vibration, like a radio or television station. Many of you are learning to align yourselves with the particular vibrations of some of these other dimensions so you can actually experience them. And when you make the connections you're able to take advantage of the teachers and the wealth of knowledge and experience that is there for you.

But how do we make that connection?

Through meditation, chanting, self hypnosis, losing yourself in certain types of music and dancing and many other methods. You're doing it right now when you meditate. One of the purposes of meditation is to quiet your mind and focus your intention on experiencing another mental state with a different vibration.

When you make the connection with me, you're tuning into my wave length, just like tuning into a radio station. Actually, we meet somewhere in the middle. Your vibration increases and mine decreases.

Do you have a body of some kind?

I am a form of energy such as light. You could say I am an idea in the mind of God or All That Is, which is the same thing. We are each an expression of this whole. You are

the embodiment of an idea from the Universal Mind that has gone forth to manifest on a physical level. You are a spark of love that is sent forth to express itself as a unique personality. And it is your purpose to create a life that embodies that love.

What a beautiful way to put it, my love. Thank you.

I sat for a long time that morning re-reading my notes and thinking about what Bob had said. The material was fascinating to me and I was thrilled to be able to talk with him like this because it felt like we were still connected. The opportunity to learn about the mystery of what happens after we die inspired me to continue writing down these conversations, although at that point, I had no idea they would turn into a book.

ℰ 6 ℛ

The Life Review

August 22, 1995

This morning I awoke from a beautiful dream in which Bob and I were on a romantic cruise to Hawaii. When I opened my eyes and realized I was alone, I could feel the emptiness deep down inside all over again. It was still hard to believe he wasn't lying next to me in bed. Eventually I threw on a bathrobe, dragged myself into the kitchen and started the coffee.

As I opened the freezer to take out something for dinner, I noticed a half gallon of Bob's favorite chocolate chip ice cream, and remembered how he usually had a big dish of it every evening. Then one day he couldn't zip up his pants and had to switch to strawberry jello. I stood there in front of the freezer trying to decide whether to laugh or cry…and finally decided to have some ice cream for breakfast.

Hi darling. I just dreamed we were on our way to Hawaii. God, is this going to get easier? I'm really getting depressed.

Don't worry, time will heal you. The more we talk, the easier this transition will be—for both of us. You're doing fine.

Do you have any idea how much the kids miss you?

Of course I do. And you're helping them get through this because you're so positive. I'm really glad you started writing down our conversations. That had to be your decision, you know. You'll be getting a lot of information, now that you're an open channel, and we all want to communicate with you.

Who is "we" ?

"We" is the Collective Consciousness, which is referred to by many names: God, the Source, the Creator, Supreme Being, Universe, Universal Consciousness, All That Is....and that's just a few of them. But they all mean the same thing. This total consciousness, of which I am a part, is composed of many individual points of view. We're like a chorus of voices where any one of us can step out for a solo whenever we choose.

Sometimes I use "we" to refer to all spirits without physical bodies. In other cases I might be referring to interested souls who are contributing ideas, knowledge or experience. Therefore, the information you receive from me comes from many different sources and is funneled to you through my spirit. There's a great deal I don't know yet, but when you ask a question, the answer just flows through me somehow.

I still have a single voice when I want to use it, but in a larger sense I'm part of the Collective Consciousness or

God. This "duality" may be difficult for you to understand—being part of the whole and an individual at the same time. Actually, you operate in the same way. You're just not as much aware of your oneness as we are, because of the apparent separateness of your physical body.

You're right, that's not an easy concept to understand. But there's a particular question I've been wanting to ask you ever since you left. When we die, do we actually go through a process in which we review our life here on earth?

Yes, I evaluated my whole life. My soul or spirit was especially pleased with the last ten years, because that's when I attained the most growth. That's when I found out what it was to really love and be loved, to receive, to have fun and to relax.

Well...at least a little.

You're right. It's hard to believe how much I'd been missing before you came into my life. And when I made the connection with my spirit guides, a lot of things changed, especially my beliefs. In fact, those experiences made it possible for us to have this communication now.

As I reviewed my life, I could see that the first 55 years were relatively easy, though emotionally shallow. I got almost everything I wanted and thought I was doing pretty well. According to society's standards, I was fairly successful and I was getting through life with a minimum of suffering. In fact, I actually believed that was the point—not just for me, but for everyone—to see how little you could suffer or struggle. Well, I found out that's not how you grow and learn.

But my biggest illusion was thinking I could ignore my feelings. And look what it took to open my heart!! I had to lose everything in order to learn about love. It's a shame that I was never capable of loving Dorka.

Well, naturally I've been wondering if you've spoken with her yet.

Yes, I have. We had a wonderful, warm reunion and she told me how relieved she was to be finished with that life. I was so wrapped up in my own problems and frustrations, I never realized how miserable she was. She'd been trying for two years to get up the courage to leave me and go live with her sister in San Francisco. Her days were spent fighting with Bruce and at night she was getting practically nothing from me. So she was only staying in the marriage because she was afraid to let go.

And why were you staying with her?

To avoid feeling guilty for not living up to my responsibilities. Also, to be perfectly honest, I didn't want to give her any money. And believe me, I had to take a long hard look at what *that* attitude cost me!

I imagine so. But, as you told me years ago, you'd never been in love, so you had no idea how happy your life could be with someone else.

That's true. The only thing I could see was financial loss. I'd still have to support her and I'd lose half of everything I had. So I justified my infidelities with the fact that there was no sex in my marriage. It never even occurred to me that I'd be doing Dorka a favor by setting her free.

First of all, I thought she wouldn't want a divorce because she was Catholic; however, now I know that she'd gladly have agreed to a separation. Obviously, we were both so terrified of change that we just hung in there until the steam kettle exploded. Since then I've learned that when we're too stubborn or fearful to make the changes that are necessary, they're created for us anyway. Dorka is a lot happier now and has already come back into another body.

Do you know where she is now?

Yes, but I can't give you that information. There are many things humans are not entitled to know because it would alter or interfere with the lives they're destined to live.

But you still haven't told me who murdered Dorka?

I haven't told you because it's still not time for you to know. As I said before, certain information is unavailable to you for various reasons. Not just in this case, but for others, too. When it's time for the mystery to be solved, you'll understand why it was necessary to wait. Do you remember when Dorka first told us we'd know the truth when it didn't matter any more?

Yes, of course. But it really doesn't matter. I'd still love Bruce just the same, whether he's guilty or innocent. You know that, don't you?

Of course, but the time for knowing the truth is not for you to decide. Dorka and I finally had an opportunity to discuss the situation at length. Primarily, we both needed to acknowledge and take responsibility for the roles we played in creating it. And I must say, we've learned a lot.

But I don't understand. It wasn't your fault.

Oh yes, I was definitely a contributing factor to the whole scenario, and so was Dorka. We both knew that Bruce was heading down the road to destruction, but neither of us was willing to accept any responsibility for his problems. As far as we were concerned, everything was his fault.

That's not to say that Bruce was blameless. But from my present perspective, I can see that the murder was the culmination of *all* our problems and our refusal to acknowledge them. I just kept putting my head in the sand and believing all of Bruce's lies because I loved him so much.

I suppose that's what a lot of parents do.

Well, I knew he was hooked on drugs, but I didn't know how bad it was. I didn't want to know. But one thing is certain—he'd be dead by now if he hadn't gone to prison. Ultimately, that's what saved his life. He's exactly where he needs to be right now—and you must trust that.

You really think Bruce would be dead by now if he wasn't in prison?

I'm sure of it. And I wouldn't have lived as long as I did either. In the final analysis, Dorka's death liberated the whole family, because we all got what we really wanted. As you know, both of us wanted out of the marriage and Bruce wanted the world to take care of him so he wouldn't have to work. Dorka told me she didn't really mind going, so the decision wasn't difficult for her. She just wanted out.

Then you're saying that whoever committed the murder did her a favor?

I know this sounds strange, but from a larger perspective, her murder actually freed her from a life she hated. You might also be surprised to learn that she *chose* not to regain consciousness before she died, purely out of love for Bruce and me. She knew that if she pronounced him guilty, Bruce wouldn't have been able to forgive himself and could never have been rehabilitated. And if she'd pronounced him innocent, he would have moved in with me and continued his drugs. And neither of us would have lived more than a few years. So *all* our lives would have been destroyed.

The ironic part of this whole tragedy is that the murder made it possible for me to enjoy the happiest years of my life, even though they were tainted with guilt and heartbreak over Bruce.

*Well, I must admit, it certainly changed **my** life for the better… and the lives of Terri and Elliot, too, because I got you as a husband and they got you as a father.*

I was disappointed about not being allowed to know the truth about the murder. But I understood that the reason had to do with the lives of those of us who were still here, and I had to trust it was for our benefit.

℘ 7 ℘

The Afterlife 101

August 28, 1995

It felt like I hadn't slept a wink all night, although I'm sure I must have dozed off at some point. I was still in a daze when I got up at 7:00 and promptly started crying. I'd been getting calls from some of Bob's clients in the past few days who said they felt lost without him. Well, so did I.

As I sat at my kitchen table drinking coffee and watching the sun streaming in through the window, I became aware of the faint smell of cigarettes and knew Bob was around me. I laughed and pulled out my notebook.

Good morning, honey. So tell me, what are you doing over there?

All the things I never had time for when I was in my body because I was too busy making money. We don't have to worry about that here. Mostly I'm sharing what I learned on earth and learning new things, but I'm also visiting all sorts of places to see what's going on.

Oh? Like what?

Like tennis matches at Wimbledon, the Taj Mahal and exploring the Amazon jungles without having to worry about insects or snakes. Everything is available, plus watching over you and the rest of the family and being there for you whenever you ask. Do you have any idea how wonderful you all are?

Thank you, Bob. I guess we don't see ourselves as you do.

I knew it when I was there, but I'm aware of it even more now, seeing how much love and sharing and caring you all have for each other. I couldn't have left Bruce in better hands, sweetheart. I have no fear that he'll be just fine — even better than when I was there.

I doubt that. You were the most important person in his life and I know he misses you desperately. But he's talking to the whole family on the phone now, not just to you and me like he did before, and I think this is good for him.

I think it's good for all of you. You teach each other, you know.

I was just wondering, Bob, do you learn things the same way we do here?

Yes. Information comes in, is understood and assimilated, then used or shared, which is very similar to your own learning process.

Where I am, however, the information comes in a little differently. We absorb whole concepts at once. Instead of separate words, the ideas are communicated in their totality—like big chunks. I call them "living informational units." I've communicated with you many times in this way. You usually need to break down these concepts into words in order to explain them to yourself and others. Does this sound familiar?

Absolutely.

. . . . . .

September 2, 1995

I took a look at my desk this morning, piled high with insurance policies and forms to fill out, and wished Bob were here to help me. Of course, if he were here, these papers wouldn't be here either. I took out my pad and the first sentence I wrote was a complaint.

I had no idea that all this financial stuff would be so complicated and time consuming. It's practically a full time job! I could sure use your help. You were always so good at this kind of thing, but to me it's exhausting! I hope I get a handle on it soon because I'm beginning to feel overwhelmed.

That's because you're resisting so much. And whatever you resist drains your energy. But don't worry, the more you dig into it, the faster you'll learn.

I suppose so, but I'd rather be learning about the kinds of things we talked about with Yallen and the Director. Remember? Maybe you and

I could do the same thing now, and you could be my teacher. What do you think?

Actually, I don't even know how much I know yet, but I guess I'll find out. I'm still learning and evolving, too, you know.

We continued our conversation with some advice from Bob about a pressing financial matter, and later that day I dug through my files for transcripts of our sessions with Bob's guides. I found several pages of dictation from his last teacher, the Director, which Bob typed himself, along with a number of conversations with Yallen, his first spirit guide, which I'm including here.

Joy: *Does the individual soul determine what its next lesson is to be?*

Yallen: Yes, each individual's development is, in a sense, predetermined. There are experiences that each spirit feels required to have and these come in an order determined by the spirit itself for its growth and its ultimate pattern in the universe. It is the spirit's need that controls and inspires the choice of experience.

Each spirit develops in its own way toward its own ultimate destiny in the universe. Once it has achieved its full growth of experience, at some point in time it can be in harmony with and part of the Universe or All That Is and finally be at rest. All spirits will

eventually reach that stage, once they have all the experiences they need from many lives.

Joy: *And who or what is All That Is?*

Yallen: It is everything and the Source of everything, including all experience. Many of you use the term God.

Joy: *So the ultimate purpose or destination is to be one with this Source?*

Yallen: That is the *only* goal, the only destination for all. Since we are all part of one spirit, our purpose is to absorb all the experiences necessary to eventually merge with that oneness.

Joy: *Then we are all in different stages of development here on Earth?*

Yallen: Of course.

Joy: *Are there really such things as heaven and hell and angels and devils—or did we just make all that up?*

Yallen: If it is necessary, a spirit will have the experience of devils, hell, angels, or heaven. When a person physically dies and believes he will go to heaven or to hell, his spirit will have that experience and it will be real to him. But it is not a necessary course for a spirit, it is only an option.

Joy: *Are you saying that we choose the experience out of our beliefs?*

Yallen: We choose it out of our need. It is not a matter of your belief as a human being. It is a matter of the need of your spirit for its own growth and understanding. But your experience of heaven or hell is not an end. Your spirit will continue on after it has taken what it needs from that experience.

Joy: *What can you tell me about people like Jesus Christ, Buddha and Mohammed?*

Yallen: They were all teachers. Jesus Christ, in his time on earth, considered himself a rabbi and a teacher; however, he was accepted by many as the Son of God. But all are the sons and daughters of God. Jesus was able to perform what was believed to be miracles, but all have the power to perform these things.

The rest of them, Buddha, Confucius, Mohammed, and millions of other teachers have all carried a message to humans to do good and to avoid evil. But none of them, with the possible exception of some of the wise men of the East, really conveyed the total idea of the oneness of the individual with All That Is. What these men taught has been changed into fear by many, which is not right.

All of us, regardless of our stage of development, can expect to become one with the Source when our growth, education and experience are completed and developed sufficiently to reach that state. You must understand that this is a continuing and never ending process. There are many behind, many ahead, many beside you, all moving toward the same gateway. And it will never end. Some may attain that goal and still return for further experience in some lifetime—beside us, ahead of us or behind us—because they may have other functions to perform once they have attained the goal of oneness.

Joy: *Is that what Jesus did...achieve that oneness and then come back here as a teacher?*

Yallen: Many of the great teachers did that. And it was not their intent to be revered. It was only their intent to teach. However, there must have been a need in each of them for the feeling that one enjoys when you receive that kind of attention from others. Therefore, it occurred. This can happen to the greatest among you. However, it does not matter because they have imparted words and deeds that are far greater and more important than those of others, and those words and deeds came from them because of their closeness to the Source.

Joy: *How do you feel about the Bible and its translations?*

Yallen: If you could read the original writings from which the Bible was created, you would have a truer understanding of what was said. They were not intended to be used as they are now. They started out as a history of events, but became changed over the years by groups and individuals for their own purposes. Even today the Bible is used to justify and validate many different beliefs by fitting it to the needs of the reader or speaker. The stories are meaningful and there is some truth in all of them. However, the truth is in the eye of the beholder, so whatever truth you wish to see, you will find it there.

Joy: *As I understand it, the original version urged people to revere God, not fear him.*

Yallen: That's correct. In the beginning, people were taught to revere and accept God. But the changes were made in the translations by people to serve their own needs.

Joy: *And when Jesus said "He who believeth in me shall find the kingdom of heaven," didn't he mean for people to believe in themselves, rather than in him?*

Yallen: He spoke in parables and the translation is not right. It should have read, "He who believeth in himself, in his own spirit...." There were many instances where the translations did not relate to the original. Jesus, of all people, would not have said anything to encourage the worship of himself.

Joy: *Was there a time when there wasn't any organized religion?*

Yallen: Of course. There was direct communication with the Source.

Joy: *Will we ever get back to that?*

Yallen: Possibly, but it is unlikely unless there are many changes among the masses of humanity. Your planet and its inhabitants are almost like babies in the universe.

Joy: *Are we making some progress?*

Yallen: A little.

Joy: *Are there other planets and places that have as much variety in their religions as we do?*

Yallen: Yes and no. There are many planets inhabited by beings that are completely different from you, with disparate forms of expressing reverence and belief. Others are inhabited by beings of such high intelligence that they do not believe in anyone superior to them, even a Creator. Some beings are in complete communication with the entire plan of creation, so they have only one belief, and it is not what you call a religion. It is a harmony with All That Is. As you are beginning to learn, there is everything in the Universe. And now I wish you good evening.

Joy: *Thank you, Yallen. It was wonderful speaking with you and I hope we can do this again soon.*

Yallen: That is why I am here.

As I read the transcripts again after so many years, I remembered how exciting it was to replay the tapes for Bob and discuss all the fascinating information we'd received. I also noticed how different Yallen's tone and choice of words were from the way Bob spoke.

I began to realize that all the time we spent talking with Bob's spirit guides must have prepared us for the experience we were having now. But how could we have ever known that Bob would eventually become *my* spirit guide!

8

What About God?

September 7, 1995

After a delightful evening of dinner and a movie with several close friends, I woke up in a great mood today, full of questions I hoped Bob would answer for me. I could feel his presence almost the minute I thought about him.

Okay, if you're really serious about my asking questions, these conversations could get pretty interesting, because I never run out of questions.

How well I know!

Well, to start with I'd like to hear what you have to say about God. Is there actually a God as most people visualize him?

If you mean some old man with a beard sitting up in the clouds judging everyone and striking you dead, no, there's no such thing. And you really can't say "him" or "her," because neither pronoun applies. Abstract

principles can be difficult to conceptualize, so we often personalize these ideas to make them more vivid and understandable.

God is probably the best example of this. The Universal Consciousness is usually depicted as a father figure, sitting up in the sky somewhere dispensing rewards and punishments. The reason for this is that human beings can easily relate to this image, because it was designed to emulate the behavior of their human fathers.

I can see how this could be a simple way to teach children about the universe since they already have a basis for understanding. But it seems like a lot of people never get beyond the image of a larger than life being they call God. So tell me, exactly what or who is God?

God is simply a term used to signify the consciousness or life force of the entire Universe. God is not separate from you. *You* are God just as much as a drop of water from the ocean is the ocean, even though it's not the whole ocean. There is no God *person* "out there."

God is the total energy of all the elements—fire, water, earth and air—and so much more. If you can visualize God as a torch, then we are all sparks from that central eternal fire. You use the word "God" for a concept that is so all-encompassing your individual minds can't really conceive of it. It's like a hologram, where the whole is incorporated in the parts. I often use the word "Universe," which gets away from the concept of a person or human being.

I am part of that central energy force now, yet I also express myself as an individual spark. I am free to do, think, feel and learn as much as I can absorb. I proceed at my own pace and my interests and desires lead me to expand further, just as you do in your reality.

Are you aware of what goes on in my reality?

I am acutely aware of many things—ideas, feelings, beauty, love, learning, other spirits, but most of all, *life* in all its forms. I'm more aware of all this than you because, whereas you are individualized or separated, I am conscious that I'm part of the whole. I can choose the state of oneness or individuality. This is called the "duality."

Another difference between us is that I'm more aware of my choices and my own power. You have the same inner power as I, within the parameters of your physicality, but the illusions imposed by your five senses tend to limit you.

What do you mean by illusions?

Although your physical senses are valuable in helping you enjoy your earthly experiences, they often create a smokescreen. For example, they present the illusion that you humans are all separate from each other, that physical death ends the life of the soul, and that time as you know it actually exists. Many other beliefs you consider to be the truth are also illusions.

Is it true that we all come back again into other lives and bodies?

Yes, but your spirit or soul remains here in this reality, accumulating all the love and knowledge from the various lives you are experiencing. And incidentally, we all live many lives at once, since time is merely an illusion.

My spirit sends out sparks of itself to experience physical lives in order to grow and progress. At the same time, my spirit itself is a spark from the Universal Consciousness, which then grows and expands as a result of my life experiences.

The best way to understand this concept is to visualize a human form with a dozen hula hoops spinning on each arm and each leg and around the torso. Now imagine that all these hoops are physical lives and that you're living all of them at the same time. Have you got that?

I think so.

Now if each of these hoops represents an individual life, time appears to move in a linear fashion as the hoop rotates. However, if you look at the whole picture from the perspective of the central figure, the way you see linear time is an illusion. Time actually moves in a spiral pattern, which is difficult for you to perceive from where you are. But remember, nothing in the universe is static.

Well, I can definitely picture the hula hoops. Thanks. That helps a lot.

After each life is completed, the only things that can be salvaged from the experience are love and knowledge. And that includes everything you love, not just people. This is all that goes into the "bank" to help the spirit grow. Nothing else has much value in the final analysis.

Reading over my notes, I was amused to hear Bob say that time as we know it doesn't really exist. I mean, here was a guy who not only insisted on punctuality, but allowed so much time for traffic jams that we were invariably *early* for everything, including dinner parties. I felt so sorry for all those flustered hostesses who practically tore their hair out when we'd arrive while they were still dressing!

· · · · · ·

September 11, 1995

About six weeks after Bob's death, I was getting into the shower one morning and began to feel a strange sense of lightness, both physically and emotionally. What really surprised me was the sensation of pure joy that was flowing through me in waves. This was the last thing I expected at that particular time in my life. Then I started losing weight.

About two weeks later I felt so happy that I began to feel guilty about it. Since I missed Bob terribly, it didn't make any sense to me at all, so I asked him to explain what was happening.

Honey, I really don't understand all these feelings of lightness and joy that have been coming over me lately. It seems like part of me is in mourning and the other part is smiling all the time. What's going on?

· 65 ·

First of all, my dear, you didn't realize how much pressure you were under as a result of my health problems. You always thought you were handling everything just fine. However, the emotional burden was literally adding weight to you. When I left, that burden was lifted and you started feeling lighter.

And that's why I started losing weight?

Exactly. You'll notice that when it comes to physical weight, most people have it backwards. They think that when they get thinner, they'll get happier. But it's actually just the opposite. When you get happier, you get thinner. When you feel good about yourself and your life, your body automatically adjusts to its ideal weight. In your case, with the worry and anxiety suddenly gone, plus knowing that I was happier than I'd been in a long time, why wouldn't you be joyful?

But it's only been a few weeks. I'm supposed to be in mourning. I never expected to be feeling all this joy and it's making me feel guilty. I'm afraid people will think it's a little weird that I'm not walking around looking miserable at least part of the time.

Honey, don't ever feel guilty about being happy.

But sometimes it just doesn't seem appropriate. It's like giggling at a funeral.

Those are just the customs of your particular culture. There are other societies—now and in past times—that celebrate the passing of a loved one with singing and dancing and laughter—like a graduation or an ascension. They understand that the spirit is going home, and they send them on their way with the pure energy of joy.

You know, that sounds terrific, but it's certainly not that way here.

Your society has a lot to learn about what you call death as well as the power of feelings. You see, when you experience joy you are in perfect alignment with the energy of love and are, therefore, in total harmony with the Universe. And whatever feelings you experience are not just affecting you, they radiate out to everyone around you. So the more joy you feel, the more joy you send out to others as a gift to the world.

Then my friends must be rather surprised at what's radiating out from me these days. So what is it we need to learn about feelings, especially joy?

First of all, the greatest joy comes from loving who you are, what you do, and who you're with. But joy doesn't always express as pleasure, you know. There can be joy in giving birth, for example, even when it's physically painful. There can also be joy in hard work if you love what you're doing, or in the struggle to master something new or accomplish a goal. If you're passionate about achieving something, every effort in that direction is part of the love and joy.

Many people never allow themselves to acknowledge pure joy. They keep postponing their happiness until some future time when they feel their life will be in order. They think that when they get married, or win the lottery, or have a baby, or lose 20 pounds, then they'll be happy.

I know. Alot of them wait until some situation outside of themselves gives them a reason to be happy.

They don't realize that happiness, bliss, ecstasy, passion, fulfillment and satisfaction are all just a states of mind, which you can choose to experience whenever you wish. All you need to do is focus on something wonderful in your life at the present time and acknowledge your joy. And rest assured, if you can't find anything to feel happy about in the present, you'll never find it in the future either. You see, there's no way for you to experience tomorrow. You can only experience today.

But what if someone's life is filled with sorrow or poverty or illness? What if you've just lost a loved one? How do you deal with that?

I'm not saying you shouldn't feel your honest and heartfelt emotions of grief, sorrow, hurt, or disappointment. You need to experience these feelings thoroughly and completely, because only then will you be able to let them go. Feelings demand your attention and must be acknowledged. Otherwise, all the unexpressed emotions and unshed tears will stay in your body and eventually form tumors, cancer and maladies of all kinds.

Tears possess enormous healing power and can be used to help cleanse and wash away the pain of negative emotions. On the other hand, tears provide an outlet or overflow for positive emotions, too, such as intense joy, passion and sentiment.

But what if someone's life is really miserable or full of tragedy?

It's impossible for a person's life to be totally filled with negative situations. There is always something positive, something to be grateful for, even if it's only having food to eat, a place to live, someone to love or good health. So it's up to you. You can sit around and worry about what's missing in your life, or you can focus on what you have to be grateful for.

Just because you don't have everything you want all at once is no reason to be perpetually unhappy. Most likely there will always be something missing in your life, and it's missing for a reason. What's there at the present time is precisely what you need to experience and learn from now.

So in the long run, happiness doesn't have to depend on the circumstances of your life, as most people think. The choice of happiness is pretty much up to you.

When I finished writing, a memory came back to me of a time many years ago when my children were small and I was struggling to make ends meet on $59 a week. It was right after my first marriage ended and, though I was barely managing to pay the rent, I still remember how happy I was. By most people's standards, I should have been scared and insecure, but I felt young and free and totally optimistic about the future.

Those joyful feelings didn't make a lot of sense to me even then, and I feel the same way now. I was relieved to know that my happiness was not a sign that I didn't care about Bob and what we had together. It's just a choice I've learned to make, no matter what's happening in my life.

৪০ 9 ᘉ

Notes From Bob's Spirit Guide

September 14, 1995

I was starting to get bored and didn't know what to do with myself, especially at night. Watching television and going to dinner with my girlfriends was getting old, so I enrolled in a ballroom dancing class. It was fun and great exercise, and at least it got me out of the house in the evenings. I began my conversation with Bob by telling him about the dancing lessons and he replied:

> **Use your imagination to create your life. This is the creative energy of the Universal mind. It works through you to form your present and your future. Don't ask for what you want. Imagine it and make it real in your mind. You are never helpless. Just remember that I want you to be happy. Your joy is a joy for me to watch and feel as you go through life.**

Sometimes his words were so beautiful they made me cry. And this was one of those times.

Thank you, my love. I just wish you were more a part of my life.

And I wish you were here with me, too, but you and I have work to do while you're still there, and that's very exciting to me. Thank you for opening up the channel to receive me and what I have to give to your world. I never felt I was giving back enough while I was there. I always felt I was selfish because I got pretty much everything my own way in that life. Of course, now I see how it works. In the long run, we all "get our own way"—even when it doesn't look like it—because we all make our own choices. In fact, from this perspective I'm seeing how a lot of things work that I never understood before.

Sounds like you're learning a lot. Will I be able to understand it?

Not all of it. Some concepts are more advanced than you can comprehend right now, but if you can stretch your mind a little, I'll share as much as possible. This is the kind of stuff the Director wanted me to get into while I was there. Remember how he used to nudge me to sit down at the computer on a regular basis and let him talk. Of course, he always said it was strictly up to me...but I was far more interested in making money and going to the races.

Yes, I know. As a matter of fact, when I was looking through some old files recently, I found some dictation you took from the Director which confirms a lot of the information you've been giving me.

Director: *We are all part of the Universe, whether in spirit form as I am or in physical form as you are, and we are each at various stages of knowledge and growth. There are billions of us, each with our own distinctive characteristics, talents and abilities different from all others. We were all created by the Universal Consciousness and have existed in spiritual form throughout eternity.*

Each time our development calls for a physical experience, we enter a body and embark on a physical life, which may be in human form on your planet or in other forms on other planets or even other galaxies. While the time of our physical life may be long or short, it is of no consequence to our spirit, since there is no time in the Universe as you know it.

The purpose of this physical experience is to allow us to complement and expand our intellectual knowledge of truth. Just as you adjust your legal work by practical experience on top of book knowledge, we do essentially the same thing. One might say that physical beings were created to give spiritual beings actual hands-on experience to reinforce the truth of the general knowledge we learn outside of the physical body.

During a physical life one is usually not aware of one's existence as a spirit. The reason is that without this awareness one may learn the lessons without being influenced by knowledge already acquired by the spirit. However, nothing is fixed and there are some who become aware of and communicate with spirits during their physical lives.

Many beings also experience flashes of knowledge from an inner source, which you call the subconscious. These insights come and go, and are intended to remind humans that they have abilities beyond those they are aware of which come from their non-physical existence. Each of you can develop and expand these flashes to facilitate further knowledge of your relationship with the Universal Consciousness.

Essentially, human beings are vehicles for the spirit within them to learn by doing—or not doing—as the case may be. For those who wish to explore the relationship between their physical and spiritual beings, the rewards can be immeasurable in personal growth and expansion of knowledge about their current life and the universe in which they exist.

When a being is in a physical state, the memories, while not gone, are buried deep in the innermost subconscious. However, the spirit retains all knowledge and memories of every physical lifetime and is privy to knowledge obtained by other spirits, which is transmitted instantaneously.

Most spiritual beings enter physical life shortly after conception, although they can enter at other times as well. When a being has completed a physical life and the body is not ready to terminate, another spiritual being will move in to take the place of the one departing. Obviously, there must be a spiritual being in the body to give it life or it will cease to function.

This type of occurrence may be impromptu as a matter of choice by the arriving or departing beings, or it may be a planned experience. If you find that someone you know has changed dramatically for no apparent reason, this may be the result of a change of occupancy. Sometimes these beings are called "walk-ins."

I hope we will talk again soon. But before I go, there's something I want to mention to you. You know logically that cigarette smoking is not good for you. You feel the ache in your chest every time you smoke a cigarette. You don't heed the Surgeon General's reports, doctor's warnings, or other advice. I will not tell you that you should or should not smoke. It may well be that you are destined to leave your physical body via lung cancer, emphysema or a heart attack.

I will not tell you to quit smoking, just as I will not tell you about probable events in your physical life. Choices are always there for you to make and each choice creates its own pattern for your future. However, if you are interested in carrying out any of your goals, I suggest you review and consider in depth your attitude toward cigarettes.

End of lecture. And now good night.

Bob was never able to stop smoking completely, although he eventually cut down from two packs a day to (I'm guessing) two or three cigarettes at the end. But it was too late to stop the emphysema that was diagnosed seven years later. He was finally forced to carry around a breathing machine everywhere he went and there were a number of panicky moments when we had trouble finding an electrical outlet to plug it in. It was a terrifying way to live.

ஸ் 10 ௳

The Eternal Circle of Birth and Death

September 14, 1995

I had some personal questions for Bob this morning and then we started talking about Bruce. He expressed his gratitude to me for taking care of Bruce's needs, especially getting together the box of clothes, food and miscellaneous items Bruce was allowed to receive in prison every three months. Bob told me how much it meant to know that someone was still caring for his beloved son, and for a few agonizing moments I actually experienced some of the grief and pain he went through while he was here. It was positively excruciating! I felt as though I would never stop crying. Finally, I dried my eyes and walked out onto the patio for a few minutes to breathe some fresh air. When I returned, I felt better and resumed my writing.

Bob, is there some way you could tell me what it's really like where you are.

I wish I knew how. You have no idea how glorious it is. Sometimes I wonder why anyone would ever want to leave. There's so much love here. In fact, that's all there is. Of course, that's all there is where you are, too—

everything else is added by humans. However, the desire for knowledge, growth and experience—even adventure and danger—is very powerful and motivates most souls to take on physical lives. Experience is highly regarded here, especially the kind you get in a physical body, such as smelling a rose, touching a kitten, tasting a mango or feeling an orgasm. Experience is the reason we long to come to earth...to put our knowledge to the test in various ways. And all physical lives are valuable, no matter how long or short or obscure. There's always much to learn.

Well, if it's so glorious there, why is everyone so afraid of death?

Because human beings think "death" is the end, whereas it's actually a new beginning. Death is simply the process of moving into another reality. That's all I did.

Most people don't realize how much similarity there is between birth and death. In both cases, the soul goes through a tunnel into the next dimension or reality. Those who have had near-death experiences almost always mention traveling through a tunnel toward the light, but the baby's tunnel is the birth canal as it moves toward the light in the process of being born. Actually, the baby thinks it's dying. Not only is it entering a completely new reality, but birth can be as physically painful for the baby as it is for the mother. Also, when the baby is suddenly cut loose from its mother, its source of life, and is forced to breathe on its own, it can be terrifying.

As far as physical space is concerned, however, you'll notice that the baby doesn't move more than a few inches in the process of dying to the old reality and being born into a new one. Yet suddenly it's in a whole new world with a brand new set of rules. By the same token, death doesn't really take you away either. You simply exist in another reality in pretty much the same "space."

But isn't the baby being released from a terribly confining space when it's born into our world? Isn't it much better off in our physical reality than in that tiny, constricting womb?

That's exactly how we feel here when you die! When you are finally allowed to leave the confines of your tiny, constricting bodies, we feel you are being set free in your spiritual home. I certainly felt a lot freer.

When you leave your body through death and move to another dimension, we feel it is infinitely more "real" than your physical world. But that's as hard for you to understand where you are now as it is for the baby in the womb.

First of all, the baby has no more conception of his mother than you have of God. To the baby, his mother *is* God, but he doesn't know he's actually part of her any more than you realize you're part of God. The baby hasn't "seen" his mother and you haven't "seen" God, yet something deep within tells both of you that there is something bigger than yourselves. However, you can't actually comprehend this concept until you leave your physical dimension, just like the baby.

Fascinating! So when I die, will we be together again?

We're together now in more intimate ways than we were before, except physically, of course.

Oh, you know what I mean. Will you be there to meet me when I cross over?

If that's what you want. We all create what we want or believe when we make the transition, just as we do with everything else in our lives. For example, if you believe you'll be met by Jesus or Buddha or Moses or your parents, that's most likely what you'll experience.

Do you know when I'm going to die?

There are usually choices at various times in your life. Therefore, I can't say exactly when you'll join me here, but in your time it will be many years. I had a choice in 1989 when I was in intensive care for seven weeks. It was primarily the love I experienced from you and the children that made me decide to stay a while longer. I also had a choice this last time, but it's usually not something your conscious mind decides in advance.

It seems like almost everyone wants to die peacefully in their sleep, but it rarely happens. Why is that?

They may *say* they want to die in their sleep, but their *belief is* that old age brings disease, illness, and weakness, as well as a multitude of aches and pains that ultimately lead to death. Most doctors unwittingly encourage these beliefs by attributing many physical ailments to old age that are actually emotionally based problems—ones that have finally manifested physically. But death doesn't need to be a painful or unpleasant experience. Since it's really no different from birth, crossing over to the next dimension can be very joyous.

Also, the funeral or memorial service should be a celebration of the individual's life, like mine was—a gathering where everyone pays tribute to the departing person and wishes him or her well. This is extremely helpful to souls crossing over, because too often they're disturbed and hindered by the grief and misery of their loved ones. They long to comfort them and are frustrated when they can't communicate. So your relatively peaceful state of mind was a great gift to me because I didn't have to watch you go through unnecessary suffering.

As long as we're on the subject, I want to ask you about suicide. Is there any kind of punishment for taking your own life?

Why? It's only an experience.

Then a person has a right to do what they want with their own body?

No, the person has a right to choose the experience. It has nothing to do with the body. The body is only a vehicle. You must understand that in the broad scheme of things, there is no more judgment of anything you do in your life on earth than if you were an actor in a play. Because that's really what you are. From our perspective, what you call reality is an illusion. For us, it's like watching a play with a message. We watch your lives and learn just as you learn from watching such movies as *It's a Wonderful Life* or *Schindler's List*.

The act of suicide, which is simply the culmination of hopelessness, is an especially dramatic way to end a life. But the greatest illusion about suicide is that most people think all their problems will disappear when they destroy the body.

And that's not true?

Not at all. Every soul is responsible and accountable for their life experiences, even after they leave the body. No matter how they die, they must ultimately resolve whatever problems they were dealing with in the physical universe—guilt, regret, anger, hatred, self loathing or abusing their body.

First they need to forgive themselves and those who have mistreated them. Then they must seek forgiveness from those whom they have mistreated. This usually means waiting until those people cross over, unless they can make contact the way we do. In the meantime, their spiritual progress is somewhat impeded until this is accomplished.

I can see why many people who commit suicide are in for a big surprise when they discover the slate hasn't been wiped clean.

True. Now plane crashes and other accidents are dramatic, too, and attract a lot of attention. However, violent deaths of this type are especially difficult for those close to the individual because of their suddenness. At least with deaths that result from a period of illness, the survivors have more time to get used to the idea and can start to let go. One of the purposes of illness is to warn our loved ones that we are leaving.

I never thought of it that way. And with suicide, our loved ones usually have no warning at all.

True. However, be aware that you all commit suicide in one way or another—some more overtly than others. There's a part of each of you, though not usually a conscious part, that decides when, where and how you will leave the body, just as you decide when, where and how you will enter it. Your soul knows when it's time for you to make the choice whether to stay or leave. Accidents sometimes happen, but they are rare. Your society tends to place blame and shame on a person who chooses to take his own life overtly. However, it is merely another choice and holds no onus for us.

When it comes to death, most people want to believe that it just "happens" to them, without any choice or responsibility. However, you are almost always given a choice—as I was—to stay or leave. Some individuals are persuaded to return to their bodies when they would

rather not because their soul knows they have more work to do. At other times, an individual may actually have been wishing to leave before death occurs.

But even when you finally understand and accept that you create your own life, you usually resist extending that responsibility to creating your own death. You want the ending to be "an act of God." You forget that there is no God separate from you. As part of All That Is, you *are* God.

Bob's words gave me a whole new perspective on death. If the soul knows when it's time to make that choice, this explains why Bob did all those uncharacteristic things the week before he left, such as calling both his sisters and taking his secretary to lunch. Then I remembered that just a few months before he died, he also signed an agreement to sell his business in case of his death or early retirement. It's astounding to contemplate how much more is actually going on inside of us than we're consciously aware of.

⅀ 11 ⅃

How Our Thoughts Create Our Reality

September 26, 1995

As I listened to the news this morning and heard them announce that USC had won their football game against UCLA, I thought about Bob. As an alumnus, he loved the Trojans and we went to all their games until his emphysema got so bad that he became anxious about finding a place to plug in his breathing machine. It broke his heart when he had to give up the season tickets he'd had for 30 years.

Good morning, honey. I hear USC played a great game last night. Or did you already know that?

I was there.

I should have known. Anyway, I've been thinking a lot about what you referred to as the "Oneness," but the concept isn't easy to understand when that's not what I actually see. I mean, from my perspective it looks like we're all separate beings with separate lives. Can you explain this to me in a way that will make it clearer?

Well, the astronaut Edgar Mitchell gave us a good example of this concept when he described his perspective of the earth from Apollo 14. He said that if you could pull back far enough—as he did—you would see the earth as one solid being, because at that distance you can't see all the small pieces or the details. Try looking at a tree from an airplane and you'll see that from that height, the tree looks solid, too, even though you know there are thousands of leaves that are constantly moving.

The same theory holds true for the universe. If it were possible to pull back far enough, you would be able to view it as one huge "being" united by an energy or life force that flows through everything.

Your physical separateness is actually an illusion. We are all tiny little pinpoints of consciousness—all valuable and necessary to the whole, like the most minute parts of your body are all necessary to the whole organism. And just as the leaves of the tree look separate, yet are all part of the tree, you are all part of the oneness called God or All That Is.

You know, I've actually thought about that when I look at the tree outside my kitchen window.

Nature is one of your best teachers. In this case, it can help you understand how human beings are connected. Each tree and plant appears to stand alone, yet their root systems are interconnected to the universal root system of all plant life on earth.

Basically, everything is nourished by the same soil. And when that soil is polluted by toxic material at any point on the globe, all the plant life on earth is affected to some degree. The same is true of the fish kingdom, whose basic element is water. When there is an oil spill, it affects the entire ocean and all its inhabitants.

Do you remember a few days ago when you said "I love you" to one of your little indoor plants and it thanked you on behalf of all your plants?

Of course. I was dumbfounded! I've always known there was an awareness in plants, but it was the first time I ever heard—or rather sensed—a reply from one.

Well, it's true that the love you give to one plant is felt by all. And when you neglect one of your plants, they all feel that, too. They're far more aware of their connectedness to each other than human beings are, but the same principle applies. When you give love to someone, everyone around you feels it. And when you send out hate, others feel that, too.

Okay, but how are we connected?

You can see how plants share the nourishment of the earth, but your own roots are not so obvious because human beings are connected through the life force in the air. The air is your basic element. Although you can survive for days without food and water, you can't live for more than a few minutes without air.

You're not aware of this connection because it's invisible to you, but you all sense it deep down inside. And eventually, when your senses become more finely tuned, you'll actually be able to see this energy or life force.

Just as fish and plant life can be threatened by the pollution of water and earth, human beings are affected by air pollution. And this pollution is not only on a physical level. It extends much further than your physical eyes can detect, because it includes everything that is sent out into the atmosphere on a daily basis by each human being.

Every thought, word, feeling, and action you generate goes out like ripples in a lake and affects the whole world. Therefore, when you send out love and joy in any form, you actually help make the world a happier, healthier place. You become healers. And when your words of encouragement help lift someone out of a depression or an angry mood, you're actually helping yourself as well as everyone else, because you're clearing out the pollution.

So does that mean when we're feeling angry and hateful, we're polluting everyone else's life along with our own?

That's correct. The whole world is the recipient of your negativity. Spewing out anger and hatred is like dumping toxic waste into the atmosphere. If you really understood your connection to the Universal Consciousness, you would have to share in the responsibility for everything that occurs on your planet.

By choosing to take action to change things, you are adding your power to those with similar beliefs. Uniting in this way is highly effective in promoting change.

That's pretty wild! So you're saying that everything I say and do affects the whole world?

That's exactly what I'm saying. Whatever you do, say, think or feel toward one person not only affects everyone in your own life but, to one degree or another, the entire universe.

For example, if you lie, cheat, steal or act without integrity, on a very basic level it will pollute your whole life. If you exude anger or hatred for your boss or ex-spouse, for example, those feelings will contaminate your most loving relationships.

Your life is not compartmentalized. That negative energy will spill over into all areas, because nothing and no one is separate. What you do to one, you do to all.

Is it true that when a large group of people put forth the same thoughts and feelings, it is especially powerful?

Yes, this is an extremely potent force that can create all sorts of interesting phenomena. And it does all the time, because a whole mass consciousness is formed from that energy.

From the sheer volume of thoughts, words, feelings or actions emanating from this mass consciousness have come incredible healings and miracles as well as disasters, crime and prejudice. Just as your own thoughts and feelings create your personal life, the combined thoughts and feelings of families, companies, cities and countries create the events of the world.

For example, imagine a city where millions of people are grumbling about the volume of traffic every morning, complaining about overcrowded conditions and wishing things were the way they used to be before so many people came pouring in. What do you suppose the results of all those feelings might be? How about earthquakes, floods, fires, and riots? That should weed out a lot of people, plus keep a few more from coming who might be considering relocating there.

Well, that's what happened in Los Angeles from the mid 80s to the mid 90s. I know because I was part of it. I was one of those people griping and complaining on my way to work each morning as I fought the traffic.

Explain to me exactly how we create this world around us?

To begin with, you all have different "realities," depending on your perspective. Do you see the reflection of the tree outside the window in the glass top of your table? That's how "real" your reality is. It's just a reflection of you, meaning your thoughts, feelings and expectations. It's simply a mirror that constantly gives back what you're giving out. This isn't theory. That's how it works. Once you really understand that, you'll be able to claim the power to create whatever you want.

And exactly how do I do that? How do I create whatever I want?

The determining factors are what you want, what you expect and what you focus on. The earth is your playground and you have everything to choose from. Everything you can possibly imagine is there, but that doesn't mean you have to choose it, of course. You can choose nothing or hide in a corner by yourself, or concentrate on one thing, or try everything. It's all up to you.

In any case, your imagination is your most powerful tool for creating your life. What you can imagine and make real in your mind is automatically created in your reality. Your thoughts, fears, ideas and beliefs are the actual building blocks of your future. It makes no difference whether you keep these inside or send them out in the world through written or verbal communication. Whatever you strongly believe, whatever you hold onto and keep repeating will automatically manifest in your life.

You may want to take a look at some of the events in your past to see how you created or attracted them into your life. You might be surprised at how subtly this law works.

This sounded interesting, so I decided to spend some time meditating on the concept. Before long I came up with several examples of how my own thoughts had manifested my reality without my conscious awareness, and how it had for others, too.

When I was 17, I visited a beautiful family with three children: two boys, a year and a half apart, and a daughter born six years later. While the boys were both in college, the 13-year-old girl and her mom were having so much fun together that I decided I wanted exactly the same kind of family. And that's what I got! Elliot and his brother Michael were 19 months apart and even though I thought I'd never have any more children after my first marriage, Terri came along six years later with my second husband. Michael died when Terri was four, but I did have that family for awhile...just as I visualized it.

Then I remembered the time my mother announced in the fall of 1968 that she thought she'd be ready to leave her body around June of the following year. It wasn't a morbid conversation—far from it. She was just bored with her life and curious about what was on the Other Side. It never entered my mind again until June 1969 when I got a call that she was in the hospital. On my way over to see her, I remembered her remark of the previous year.

The minute I walked into her hospital room, mother informed me that the doctors had run dozens of tests and still couldn't find out what was wrong with her. So I reminded her of the prediction she'd made, and suggested that her subconscious was simply following orders.

Now my mother was extremely knowledgeable about metaphysics—she'd been my teacher, for god's sake!—but sometimes she had trouble acknowledging how she created certain situations in her own life. Like this one! When they sent her home three days later, the doctors still didn't have a clue about the cause of her problem. And she lived another six years!

There was also a rather bizarre incident that happened about six months ago regarding my license plates. One day I started thinking about ordering a personalized plate, but I wasn't sure how to go about getting one. It didn't cross my mind again until the following week when I walked into the carport and noticed that both my plates were missing. Someone had unscrewed the frames and stolen them! I had to laugh, remembering what I'd just been wishing for.

When I went to the DMV the next day, I asked for a plate that read JOYOUS 1, but it was already taken, along with 2, 3, 4, and 5. So I settled for JOYOUS 6 and joked to the clerk that people might think it was Joyous Sex, even though at the time Bob and I weren't having any sex at all, due to his poor health. But as fate would have it, my license plate eventually came true, as you'll find out later in this book.

Thanks, Bob. That was fascinating to go back and notice the connection between thoughts, desires and life experiences. I guess when we take an honest look at cause and effect, the events of our lives seem pretty obvious. It's just that most of the time, we forget to connect the dots, so nothing ever looks like our fault.

You might also want to take a look at what your life is comprised of now, because that's what you've been choosing. You may not realize that *you* are doing the choosing, but whatever is there, you've chosen it on some level. And not only do you *create* your reality, you *are* your reality. Nothing is ever forced on you. Nothing is ever kept from you. You are the magnet that attracts or repels everything. Once you accept this, you can take control of your destiny. *Real* control is knowing you have choices every moment of your life.

I hadn't realized how much my thoughts, words, actions and even my state of mind affected the whole world. That really made me stop and think. As I reviewed what Bob had said, it looked like the good news is that our life is our own creation, and the bad new is that there's no one else to blame.

ଚ 12 ଔ

Spirit Guides and Angels

September 29, 1995

This morning Bob and I spent some time discussing the trip to Egypt I was planning to make in November. It was a two-week tour of Cairo and the pyramids with some Egyptian tour guides, as well as a cruise down the Nile to visit the ancient temples. As a result of our conversation, I began thinking about spirit guides and remembered that I wanted to ask Bob some questions on this subject.

Honey, would you please explain to me exactly what spirit guides are?

Certainly. Guides are spirits without physical bodies who are in different dimensions or realities than you. They are like mentors, protectors, advisors and guardian angels.

Are you one of my guides now?

Yes, I guess you could say that.

How are guides different from angels?

Originally they were all called angels. "Guides" is a fairly recent word, in the past 50 years or so. Angels are actually the helpers or messengers of the universe, since they can materialize into physical form and perform acts of rescue or what you consider miracles. A guardian angel was the original term for a guide that belongs only to you.

What is a guide's job?

They act as spiritual parents and help you fulfill your purpose in life. They love you like a parent loves a child but, unlike most parents, they never push you or make decisions for you. Basically, they respond to your requests for assistance and information. They may nudge a little or make a suggestion, but it's you who makes the decisions and determines your own readiness by your questions and desires.

Sometimes if they know you're ready to progress, they help create situations that force you to change or let go of something or someone. This is because most people are afraid of change. They're afraid that things will get worse. They have little faith in the future.

Do guides always come when we ask for them?

Yes, they're always with you, but they don't always have your attention. They have to wait to be called on. And they *want* to be called on. Assisting you is their main job and their purpose. Some people see them, some hear them, some sense them, some even smell them.

I could relate to that because on several occasions I'd smelled cigarettes in the house when no one was smoking. Naturally, I always thought of Bob, and finally I realized that was exactly what he wanted. He was trying to let me know he was around.

I've noticed how you try to get my attention with the smell of cigarettes.

That's true. Some people hear their guides but think it's "just their imagination." Their messages often feel like an inspiration, a sudden realization or understanding, and sometimes a hunch. The more you communicate with them, the faster you learn to tell the difference between their messages and your own thoughts.

For example, right now you're surrendering your conscious, thinking, reasoning mind and letting us express through your open channel. An open mind has no barriers or limitations compared to the logical mind, which always tests new ideas by running them through the beliefs and facts a person subscribes to.

A guide's purpose is to encourage and comfort you, and to be the most perfect parent imaginable—the kind you all expected your earth parents to be and probably never were. Guides can handle the role more easily because they never judge you. They love you unconditionally and want only the best for you.

How many guides do we have?

Most people have more than one personal guide, usually two. Sometimes it's a spirit with whom they've had a physical incarnation, such as a friend or relative. As you grow and evolve you can graduate to more advanced guides and teachers if you wish. You may even ask for specific ones. Your personal feelings of readiness and worthiness usually determine the level of your guides.

Besides your personal guides, there may be a spiritual teacher as well, like the Director was for me. Your own beliefs and needs determine who your guides will be, sometimes without you even realizing it.

Your guides are with you through everything, but for centuries few people have understood that. This will change as more of you learn how to contact us.

I must say that sometimes I wonder if I'm just sitting here talking to myself. How do I know that I'm really speaking to you?

Why do you humans put so little value on "talking to yourself," as though you're the last person who knows anything? Think about that. You trust your conscious mind to figure things out, but when it comes to spiritual issues, you look for someone or something else outside yourself to supply the answers. You have all the answers within you, and you know that.

Whether you're speaking *with* God or *as* God, when you melt into the whole, or the Oneness, you *are* God. So you're actually talking to yourself anyway.

Eventually we want you to own the information you receive, in order to understand and accept your own connection to the Source, rather than attributing all your wisdom to Yallen or Bob or the Director or some other guide.

Even though our conversations may help bring you to the answers, every inspirational thought you have doesn't necessarily come from me or your guides, you know. Besides, I may not be dictating all this information to you forever. You are endlessly wise in your own right. Unwrap that wisdom, take it out into the light and trust it.

Okay, my love. Thank you.

As I wrote the last two paragraphs, I felt tears of truth welling up behind my eyes and by the time I finished, they were spilling down my cheeks. I often feel this when I've come across something that hits home, so I knew I needed to look at what Bob had just told me. It's hard enough for any of us to understand our direct connection to the Source, but to accept that we are also part of that Source is even more difficult. It's simply a matter of ceasing to play humble and claiming our own divine wisdom and power.

೮ 13 ೲ

How to Attract Money & Repel Fear

October 7, 1995

I was in a rotten mood this morning, and even though I knew I couldn't hide it from Bob, I needed to talk to him. I was getting so confused and discouraged trying to untangle all the financial details of settling his estate, that I remembered once again why I always tried to avoid things like insurance, investments and IRAs.

Honey, I haven't got a clue about any of this stuff. I guess I just thought I'd never have to deal with all these financial matters.

> **Well then, maybe it's time to pull your head out of the sand and learn about them. In fact, maybe that's what we need to talk about this morning—money and finances.**

You know, I've always thought that one of the greatest secrets of happiness and self-fulfillment is to be able to make a living at what you love. But on top of that, is there anything wrong with wanting to be rich?

Absolutely not. And if you believe there is, you'll have trouble attracting money all your life. Money itself is neither good nor bad. So to attract it to you, think of money as good, useful and beneficial. If you think of it as dirty, evil, or base, you're telling the Universe you don't want to be associated with money or soil your hands with what some people call "filthy lucre."

You also repel money by categorically judging wealthy people as greedy, corrupt, unscrupulous, or pretentious. If you really believe this, obviously, you wouldn't want to be in the same category with any of those disgusting millionaires. And the universe will dutifully comply with your wishes.

People have within them an innate desire to contribute something of themselves and to be acknowledged for it. Money is the direct reward for your personal contribution to the world. The more you love your work and feel you deserve to be paid well for it, the more money you'll attract.

But money isn't the only reward. So if you're looking only at money intake, you're missing out on all the other kinds of rewards you receive in life for your contributions. For example, one of the most important rewards is satisfaction, which could result from helping others, creating works of art, inventing or discovering something, challenging yourself in mental or physical areas, and a thousand other ways of expressing who you are.

The problem occurs when you separate money from contribution. If you want to make a million dollars, for example, ask yourself what you can contribute to the world that would bring you a million dollars. You will find the answer to that question by following what you love.

Everyone has genius in some area, and whatever you love is where that genius lies. We all need impetus to carry on, and love is the greatest impetus there is. It's not enough to just be good at something. Love is what will carry you through those difficult days and nights to achieve greatness. You see, when you know you're good at something, you feel worthy of the financial rewards that come as a result of your contribution.

That's really beautiful, honey. But what if I do something stupid and make huge investment mistakes and louse everything up? I seem to be filled with a lot of fear about all this financial stuff.

You're fearful because you're in unknown territory and you don't feel safe. But all this was second nature to me, so I'll always be here to help you. It's not that you aren't intelligent, you're just not interested in these things. When you get out of your head and start listening to your feelings, you'll sense my approval or disapproval as you go along. And eventually you'll learn to trust your instincts.

It seems like we're always dealing with fear of some kind and it stops us from doing so many things we want to do, or need to do. What's your answer to that?

Well, to begin with, your media is constantly warning you that you're not safe from anything. Every time you pick up the newspaper, turn on your TV set, read your mail or talk to your neighbors, you're inundated with dire warnings about everything from AIDS, cancer, accidents and death, to financial loss, theft, earthquake, floods, or famine. Everyone seems to love talking about catastrophes and to point out that any one of them could befall you when you least expect it.

Many of your advertisers sell products by instilling fear and doubt. And when they finally convince you that you're not as safe, secure, healthy, beautiful, young, happy or smart as you could be or should be, then you're willing to buy their insurance, burglar alarm systems, survival kits, car alarms, beauty aids, and self-help programs.

After all, if you *know* you're safe and your self-esteem is strong and healthy, you probably don't need what they're trying to sell. But most people carry around so much doubt about their safety and security that they become vulnerable to negative suggestions and all the "what ifs" that trigger their worst fears.

So why is fear even a part of life to start with?

Fear plays an important role in ensuring your physical survival. Without it you'd have no internal warning system that something was dangerous. That's why you teach your children a certain amount of fear by pointing out specific things that could hurt them, such as cars in the street, animals that bite, fire that burns, and strangers who could harm them.

Is there any reason to fear where you are?

No, because I have nothing to lose. There is no win or lose here. I have access to everything because I *am* everything, without limitation. For example, I can't lose love because I *am* love. However, once you have a body, you understand that it can be destroyed. So fear is built into you for the purpose of survival, because you can't live on earth without a physical body. Of course, your soul knows it is eternal and can never die. It can only return to the Source of All Things, or God.

Why do they say that we tend to attract what we fear the most?

You might assume that fear repels and love attracts, since you usually wish to avoid what you fear and want more of what you love. However, this isn't the case.

Fear is energy and it operates like a magnet to attract the very thing you fear. Therefore, whatever you fear becomes a distinct possibility when you focus enough energy on it. This is because whatever it is that you continually focus on, or give your attention to, is automatically magnetized into your life. By the same token, what you give no energy to is automatically repelled.

The most detrimental aspect of fear is that it keeps you from becoming all you can be—especially fear of criticism, failure, incompetency, loss, pain, illness, struggle, and poverty. Therefore those who have the most confidence and courage to stick their necks out the farthest make the most progress, fulfilling their dreams and even surpassing them. The fearful ones march in place and play it safe. They tell themselves there are already enough singers, actors, doctors, lawyers or teachers in the world, so their contribution isn't really needed.

But sometimes the competition just seems overwhelming.

There's no such thing as competition. No one else in the world can walk *your* path, so how could you ever compete with anyone? That path is yours alone, to climb as high as you want and stop whenever you choose.

Granted, the stakes get higher, the challenges more intense, the decisions and sacrifices more difficult when you go all the way. But it's strictly up to you. In fact, *everything* is up to you—how far you go and how much of yourself you're willing to experience and share with the world.

You only grow by constant cycles of reaching and stretching, followed by what feels like winning or losing. But don't be afraid of falling down once in a while. That's necessary, too, because it helps you adjust your course. That's how you learn what works and what doesn't. That's how you learned to walk, by falling down and getting up again. Nobody could do that for you. And they can't live your life for you, either. They can only stand by and cheer. That's what your parents did, and that's what your guides and angels are *still* doing.

Well, it's comforting to know that we're not struggling through this life alone.

ஐ 14 cs

How to Recognize Your Life Path

In November I went to Egypt with my daughter, Terri, my daughter in-law, Kate, and my friend, Jackie. And it changed my life. The tour, which consisted of a week in Cairo and a second week cruising down the Nile, was called *Life, Death and Beyond*. This almost turned out to be prophetic, since Jackie had a near-death experience as a result of her asthma. She actually died for 25 minutes and came back to life!

When we arrived at the Temple of Horus in the little town of Edfu on the Nile river, the combination of heat, dirt and horses was so overwhelming that Jackie began having trouble breathing. It got so bad that she finally resigned herself to the fact that she was meant to die in Egypt and she just let go. Later she told us how incredibly easy that was.

When they got her to a small clinic nearby, Jackie still wasn't breathing and had turned completely blue. The doctor was ready to pronounce her dead on arrival but Linda, the owner of the tour company and an ex-emergency room nurse, wasn't about to give up. Obviously panicked at the thought of someone actually dying on her *Life, Death and Beyond* tour, she kept shouting at the poor doctor to keep trying to revive her.

Jackie had always been skeptical about the possibility of life after death, but while they were working on her she remembers feeling wrapped in the arms of what she called the Great Spirit and surrounded with love. Then she felt herself being carried to a temple and laid on a prayer stone where hooded monks circled around her, chanting prayers. Meanwhile, back at the Temple of Horus, eighty people from the tour were standing in a circle around the horizontal prayer stone in the middle of the inner sanctum, chanting and praying for Jackie.

After not breathing for 25 minutes, Jackie suddenly sat bolt upright and yelled "What the fuck's going on here?!" while everyone in the room fell back in shock at this uncharacteristic outburst.

I have no doubt that her spirit heard our prayers and that's what kept her connected to this life. Not only did she come through the ordeal with no after-effects, she now seems even younger and healthier than before. When I asked her what she learned from her near-death experience, she told me that the Great Spirit kept saying, "Love is all that matters. And that's all there is."

I've never had a near-death experience myself, but this one was close enough to confirm my beliefs about life after death, and validate even further my connection with Bob.

· · · · · ·

I'd been getting restless and a little depressed in my condo in the Valley where Bob and I had made our home for 11 years, and was thinking about moving back to Brentwood or Santa Monica near the beach, where I'd lived before our marriage. Bob and I discussed this before I left for Egypt and he suggested I might feel differently when I came back from my trip. Nevertheless, I called a real estate agent in January and started house hunting.

February 13, 1996

Bob, I'm getting very discouraged. I can't seem to find any place as beautiful and spacious as I already have.

> Why don't you consider redecorating? It's a shame not to utilize the incredible energy that you and I created here. This place is filled with love, you know. In a new home you'd probably have to start all over to create the kind of energy you already have right here. Think about it. You might find it very stimulating and enlightening to express your inner self through your surroundings.

Hmm. I don't know. I'm not even sure what that would look like.

> Then it's time to find out. Start visualizing the kind of decor and styles that attract you—that would be the most perfect expression of you.

That sounds wonderful...and totally self indulgent!

> There's nothing wrong with thinking about yourself and expressing the beauty of who you are. In fact, that's one of the new paradigms of the Aquarian Age: *be yourself and please yourself.*

But haven't we always been taught that unselfishness is one of the highest virtues?

> Not if it means denying who you are and what you stand for. That's all you have. And in order to be yourself, you

must also please yourself. Jesus never told you to place others' needs and desires above your own. He said you should love your neighbor *as* yourself, not *more* than yourself. And not just because it's a nice thing to do either. It's because you are all one being. Others *are* you. You all come from the same fabric, even though your outer garments look different.

Giving to others always feels so good, though.

And it's certainly admirable, but when giving to others involves abandoning yourself and your own dreams, it's called sacrifice. And sacrifice is an outworn concept that has sent millions of brilliant, talented people to their graves angry, frustrated, and bitter. When all your choices and decisions are based on pleasing others, while ignoring or denying your own desires and goals, you are telling the Universe that everyone else's life is more important than yours.

That sounds like a martyr, doesn't it?

It does. You see, holding back any part of yourself from being expressed restricts your aliveness. And when this happens, you become sick and depressed. By denying or rationalizing your feelings, you sabotage your relationship with yourself as well as others. After all, if your life is not based on the truth of who you are, you are living a lie.

The formula is simple:

> **1. Listen to your heart and try to balance what you want with what others want.**
>
> **2. Honor your dreams and desires and let them lead you to your own special path in life.**

The path you've chosen for your life always involves what you love, so when you deny your basic desire nature, you deny your purpose in life. When you feel in your heart and soul that you must dance or sing or teach or write or heal people, if it doesn't hurt anyone else, follow that feeling. It's there to guide you.

By pleasing yourself, following your passion and doing what you love, you are contributing your most valuable gifts to the world. When you're happy with yourself, you automatically radiate those feelings to the people around you. And then they flourish in your positive energy, just like plants flourish in an atmosphere of love and peace. Remember, it's up to you to make yourself happy. No one else has been assigned to that job.

Wouldn't it be amazing to live in a world where everyone was busy doing what they love most!

Your world is coming to that in the New Age!

. . . . . .

When I returned from Egypt, I kept getting a message in my meditations to purchase a statue or a picture depicting Isis, the Egyptian goddess of love, beauty and femininity. For some reason, though, I kept resisting. I never mentioned this to anyone, but one morning my daughter-in-law, Kate, called to say she'd seen a beautiful statue of Isis at a local shop and thought I should have it. As I hung up the phone, I remember thinking that if she liked it so much, why didn't *she* buy it? Knowing Kate's extraordinary psychic abilities, I kept wondering what she knew that I didn't.

As fate would have it, the very next day I found myself at that shop almost by "accident." And suddenly there was Isis in all her glory—15 inches high with a 20 inch wingspan. Her wings, in the richest hues of blue, red and gold, seemed to be inviting the whole world into her arms.

Kate was right—I should have it. But when I looked at the price tag, I decided to wait. The following week I came across the same statue in another store for $100 less and realized the Universe was trying to get me to act. It was time to stop procrastinating.

Isis immediately became the focal point of my home. I decided to take Bob's advice about redecorating and his words became my mantra: "Fill this house with love and beauty."

So I began making plans to transform my condo into an Egyptian palace. I started by placing Isis on the black marble pedestal in our entrance hall that had previously held Bob's beloved bronze statue, Remington's "Mountain Man." And it was no coincidence that the marble pedestal exactly matched Isis' base.

In the next five months our conventional contemporary decor gave way to luxurious ivory couches, chairs, and carpets against pale blue walls and billowing curtains, echoing the spacious expanse of sand and sky. All this was accented with touches of gold in Egyptian styled lamps, mirrors, plaques and accessories. By summertime, I would be living in the palace of my dreams.

. . . . . .

February 23, 1996

Bob, are you aware of the major events going on in this world, such as presidential elections, natural disasters, scandals, the World Series and things like that? And are you interested?

> **Sometimes. But what you may not know is that the lives of famous people and major events that are played out on the world stage contain valuable lessons for all of us in the various dimensions. They are an excellent illustration of cause and effect. In fact, this is how you learn some of your most important lessons.**
>
> **An enormous scope of possibilities occur from the seeds of human emotions such as love, hate, prejudice, greed, faith, anger, jealousy and passion. Every person and event you see on TV or read about in the paper has become newsworthy as a result of basic human qualities and emotions taken to an extreme.**
>
> **When a life or an incident in a person's life is played out on the world stage, the ultimate purpose is often for the education, enlightenment, or advancement of the population as a whole, or for those in a particular country or community.**

Then world events can be valuable teachers for us?

Absolutely. Religious wars, the Holocaust, Watergate, race riots, AIDS, the abortion controversy, political issues, and sex scandals all demonstrate the effects of your mass belief systems, as well as your moral values and prejudices.

Famous celebrities who play out their lives in front of the public demonstrate human strengths and weaknesses for all to see, from O.J. Simpson, Princess Diana and the Royal Family, Michael Jackson, Madonna, Mother Theresa, Jesus Christ and Donald Trump to the Hillside Strangler, Jim Jones and Charles Manson. Each of these people and events has affected your world for a specific reason at a time when a specific lesson was needed to move your society further along.

Mother Theresa's life is a good example. She is the very essence and embodiment of the Piscean Age and one of our greatest role models for serving, sacrificing and denouncing the world of material values. Although she loves her work and it fills her with joy, a different type of person would consider it drudgery. She's said many times that this calling isn't for everybody.

On the other hand, the violence instigated by Jim Jones and Charles Manson were a warning to beware of cult leaders who are primarily interested in power and adulation, rather than the well being of their followers. The same can be said for some of your most famous religious leaders in the past decade.

Have you seen or talked to any famous people since you've been on the other side?

No.

Why?

I never thought about it.

Would I be able to communicate with any famous people?

Only if they also wished to speak with you. The desire has to come from both sides. It's a little like making a phone call to someone where you are. But you see, they're not celebrities here. Those were only the sparks from their essence or spirit.

Well, what about Hitler?

Hitler's job was to present the devastating effects of prejudice on the world stage, and demonstrate where those judgments can take the human race. As a result, there was probably no one in the history of your planet that was hated by so many. Would you want that job?

Hell no!

Then reserve your judgments. You are all playing the roles assigned to your spirit by the Universal Consciousness—with your agreement, of course.

This was a powerful conversation for me as it brought up issues I'd never considered before. When I discussed it later with a couple of friends, they were as stunned as I was and found it hard to accept. I remembered that Bob said we wouldn't be able to understand some of the concepts from the limited perspective of our human lives—and maybe this was one of them.

ℰℴ 15 ℭℛ

New Paradigms of the Aquarian Age

March 4, 1996

I'd found several places in my neighborhood to go ballroom dancing in the past few months and was really enjoying myself, especially after I'd gotten to know some of the regulars. When one of the men invited me to an afternoon tea dance on the famous Queen Mary in Long Beach, I accepted. Afterwards we stopped for dinner and while I was looking at the menu, I casually asked him how long he'd been divorced. Imagine my surprise when he replied, "I'm not divorced. I'm still married."

"Then what are you doing out with me?" I demanded.

"My wife doesn't dance."

Huh?! He explained that they had "sort of an open marriage," but I suspected it was only open for him.

Good morning, honey. I'm curious to hear what you have to say about my date last night. It was certainly a shock to me!

I hate to admit it, but I did the same kind of thing when I was there, you know. And so have a lot of other men. Just put yourself in his wife's place and see how you'd

feel if it were happening to you. I can see from where I am now that the Golden Rule is truly the basis for a good life, because whatever you put out comes right back to you like a boomerang. So tell me, have you thought about why you attracted this situation?

Well, not really.

Maybe you just wanted someone to take you dancing or out to dinner whom you didn't have to sleep with.

Hmmm. I thought about that for a moment and decided he might be right.

I guess I just wanted to go dancing without any strings attached. I must not be ready for a real relationship yet.

Then just dance with him at the old familiar places and be friends. Remember, you're in control of the situation.

Thanks, honey. I guess there's no harm in that. Now for the subject I really wanted to hear about today. Would you please tell me more about the Aquarian Age? You mentioned it briefly a few weeks ago, but I'm sure you have more to say.

Although most of you have heard of the Aquarian Age, if you're not familiar with astrology, you probably have no idea what it means. So I'd like to give you a little background before you read what Bob had to say on the subject.

The Aquarian Age is part of a grand cycle of 25,800 years, which is the length of time it takes for the earth's axis to complete a full circle as it moves backwards through the 12 signs of the celestial zodiac. As a result of the earth's movement, our civilization experiences the qualities and characteristics of each astrological sign for about 2200 years. In the past 5,000 years, our recorded history has been strongly influenced by the signs Aries and Pisces and we are now approaching the Age of Aquarius. Here's what Bob had to say on the subject.

The Aquarian Age will officially begin in 2012. Although you are just completing the Age of Pisces, which began around 200 BC, the transition from one Age to the next takes approximately 100 years. Therefore, your civilization has been experiencing this transition since the beginning of the 20th century.

Aquarius rules the element of air, so during the next 2200 years you will be discovering the vast potential of the air on your planet. You've already begun this, of course, with the advent of electricity, telephones, radio, television, airplanes, space travel, and the Internet.

Aquarius also rules the mind, and in the last century you've begun to explore the human psyche through the study of psychology, hypnosis, intuition and the power of the subconscious. But you are only scratching the surface when it comes to understanding your mental capabilities.

Your adventures into the inner galaxies of the human mind will be even more spectacular and earth-shaking than your explorations to other planets. In fact, one day

many people will be able to contact their loved ones in other dimensions and continue their relationships, just as we are doing. All of us on both sides will benefit from these connections, since we constantly learn from each other no matter what dimension we're in.

Then maybe we'll learn more about how to make contact with our higher mind?

There is no "higher mind," just the Mind. You gain access to it through the doorway of your own consciousness and expand into the Cosmic Consciousness—or God—of which we are all a part.

I guess I was talking about our soul or spirit.

That's a different matter. Your contact with the Cosmic Consciousness or the Universal Mind is through your spirit, which has access to all knowledge. But remember, you can only absorb that which you can comprehend.

So what can you tell me about the Piscean Age, which we've been going through for the past 2200 years? Of course I know that Pisces is a water sign and that it represents spirituality, compassion, unselfishness, sacrifice, empathy, nurturing, and unconditional love. But it also rules victimization, blind faith, superstition, fear, illusion, psychic abilities, secrets, confusion and deception. So from your perspective, how did these qualities manifest themselves during the Piscean Age?

Well first, you charted all the lakes, seas and oceans on the face of the earth. You discovered new continents and built ships to connect your far-flung societies so you could learn from each other. You discovered the truth about your planet's place in the solar system—that it revolved around the sun, not vice versa, and that it was round instead of flat. You cleared up a mountain of confusion and superstition about the world you live in and changed many of your old belief systems.

Then you began to recognize and develop your sensitivity and compassion and to value your emotional and spiritual natures. You also learned the virtues of unselfishness and how to care for each other. Instead of destroying the sick and mentally retarded, you built hospitals and institutions and formed charities dedicated to helping victims of war, disease and disasters.

So that was progress, wasn't it?

Yes, except that in the process you began to feel so good about yourselves when you started giving instead of taking, that you became addicted to having a segment of society who were needy so you could feel powerful.

As a result, you developed caste systems, slavery and social structures to ensure there would always be someone to look down on, take advantage of, or feel sorry for who would need your help. Prejudice was rampant and equality was almost non-existent until the last hundred years.

As your need for spirituality increased, you organized new religions and shifted from the worship of many gods to one God. You built churches, temples, mosques, and synagogues by the thousands, and gave parishioners new rules to live by, as set forth in the Holy Scriptures of a variety of new faiths, principally Christianity.

Eventually, as religious leaders began to wield their power, they demanded that members accept the tenets of their churches with blind faith, no questions asked. And when they discovered it was easier to control people who are unhappy and dissatisfied, they threatened them with hell and damnation as a means of control and punishment.

Then they proclaimed that the only entrance to heaven was through sacrifice, poverty, humility, and strict adherence to the laws of the church. They instilled fear, guilt, and unworthiness, as well as the belief that all human beings are born sinners. They forced their flocks to kneel and prostrate themselves before altars of gold and holy men who held the keys to their fate.

The masses were considered ignorant peasants who were unable and unworthy of comprehending the secret doctrines of the religious elite. And they accepted their lowly roles with characteristic Piscean humility.

Your religions preached that money and power were evil and sex was dirty and shameful. These beliefs were enough to keep most of the population poor, frustrated, guilt ridden and under control for quite a few centuries! You justified your religious wars and defended your beliefs at all costs with the conviction that there was only one path to God—meaning, whichever one you happened to be fighting for.

As you come to the end of the Piscean Age, you are beginning to create a new paradigm honoring individuality, creativity, equality, originality, passion, self expression, and independence—everything that makes each person a unique and valuable form of the God energy. You are finally learning how to be yourselves and please yourselves!

You'll also learn how to make yourselves happy, find your bliss and revel in it. You'll learn how to claim your divinity and equality with all mankind and realize there is absolutely no difference between the value of a peasant and a king. They are merely doing different jobs in order to learn different lessons. In other words, we are all One. Jesus and other great teachers have told you this before, but you didn't believe them.

Wow, Bob! Don't sugarcoat it! You have some pretty strong opinions.

No, just observations.

Well, thanks for the overview. It was certainly enlightening!

ℰ 16 ℛ

Change: The Only Absolute

May 20, 1996

Things were still hectic while my condo was being torn apart and redecorated from the ground up, so Bob and I weren't connecting as much as usual. My friend and decorator, Brina, held my hand, kept me focused, and even moved in with me for a month. But when the painters took over, Jackie and I took off for New York, Atlanta, and Williamsburg, and after that, I flew to Europe for two weeks with my son and his wife.

When I finally returned to my newly-painted, but near empty condo, I felt disoriented, disorganized and totally out of control. I desperately needed some order and direction in my life, but what I needed even more was someone to listen to me whine and complain. And who better than Bob?

You know, I had no idea when I started all this redecorating that it would be such a hassle! Here I am with no carpet, no drapes, and no furniture because everything's still being made. It's such a mess around here that most of the time I can't even meditate!

Whoa, slow down. You're supposed to be having fun. I thought you were going to enjoy this.

Suddenly I felt ashamed and ungrateful. It was the first time in my life that I'd been able to decorate a house exactly the way I wanted, down to the smallest detail, and here I was complaining because things were a little messy and inconvenient.

You're right, honey. I really am enjoying it—at least most of the time. And I'm very grateful for this opportunity. It's just that sometimes change can be traumatic, even when it's positive like this one. But don't worry, I'll get through it. I usually handle change pretty well, so I don't understand why it's disturbing me so much now. Maybe that's what I need to talk about this morning.

Well to start with, change is the only absolute in the universe. Meaning it's the only thing you can really count on. But you've been going through a lot of it in the last year and it's much more stressful than you've realized.

Actually, most people are more afraid of change than anything else because it involves the unknown. That's why you usually try to change other people first. The *last* thing you want to change is *yourself*, which is understandable. It requires a lot of effort and determination to alter your habits, lifestyle, attitudes, and beliefs. But when these change, the results are automatically different. They have to be.

Most of you sit around waiting and hoping for your lives to be magically transformed, yet you're unwilling to make even the smallest change to start the process. You keep doing the same things, thinking the same thoughts, and clinging to the same beliefs...then wonder why your

lives aren't turning around. For some reason, you keep expecting different results from the same cause. But the cause is always you.

Your life is created by cause and effect, meaning you are the cause and your life is the effect. And the root cause of everything is your *intention*. Each time you put forth the same intention or cause, you're choosing the same effects or consequences. However, when you put out a new intention, you're choosing new effects.

When you finally decide to take responsibility for being the cause of everything in your life, you take *control* of your life. As long as you're playing victim, feeling that everything just "happens" to you, you're coming from effect rather than cause. And when you do that, you give up all your power.

But don't things just "happen" to us sometimes? Aren't we victims of circumstances once in awhile? Like my neighbor who was mugged a few weeks ago in a parking lot. How do you explain that?

There is something in your neighbor that attracted the experience. The real cause is usually a belief or fear of some kind, although it's quite unconscious. You see, every experience you have is the result of who you are, even though some people go through their whole life pretending they don't cause anything.

They either blame others for their problems, or they just make them God's fault. They stubbornly resist new ideas and directions and then feel frustrated when their lives either stay the same or are suddenly shaken up beyond their control.

They punch a time clock for minimum wage in a job they hate, rather than quit and look for something better. They stay in miserable relationships because they're terrified they won't find someone else.

They're so afraid to actually make the changes they're praying for, that they're willing to live in the dark forever. But as long as they keep doing the same things and thinking the same thoughts, the effects will keep on looking pretty much the same.

Sort of like using the same old recipe for corn bread and then suddenly expecting it to taste like chocolate cake.

Exactly. Of course, the easiest changes to make are those prompted by love. As a result of a loved one's interest, suggestion or encouragement, you could find yourself involved in all sorts of wonderful new ideas, habits or even belief systems you might never consider on your own. With love comes trust. And the more unconditional the love, the greater the trust.

I can relate to that. Both Terri and Elliot have led me into areas of music that I'd never be involved in without them. I mean, how many senior citizens get to hang out at rock concerts? It's been a fabulous experience in my life.

The best place to start is with small changes because they inevitably lead to big ones. But first, you have to be willing to step out of your comfort zone—to stretch, to test, to risk, to choose a new attitude or intention and open up to new experiences. You won't like all of them, but the ones that feel right will take you in new directions that will make your life start to feel different.

This is not a static universe, so when you flow with the changes in your life instead of resisting them, you stay in harmony with the rhythm of the cosmos. Change is vital for growth, since without it everything withers and dies. This is as true in human life as it is in nature.

It does little good to resist the onset of winter or spring—or the seasons of your life. Therefore, learn to welcome change rather than fear it, because change is always a sign of progress and growth.

It all sounded very lofty and philosophical, but obviously some changes are extremely difficult and even traumatic—like getting used to living without Bob. However, I was finally beginning to see the truth of that old saying—when one door closes another one always opens. Bob had given me the opportunity for a whole new kind of relationship with him. And it was pretty amazing!

ஐ 17 ௯

Secrets of Effective Parenting

July 24, 1996

With the redecorating finally completed, I was having fun showing off my new home. The ambiance turned out to be so harmonious and inviting that visitors said they found it hard to leave. And so did I. I guess Bob really knew what he was talking about.

I had a lot of mixed feelings when I woke up this morning. It was a year since Bob's "graduation," as I liked to call it, and as I sat at the kitchen table drinking coffee, I was remembering what a beautiful celebration his memorial service had been.

Practically everyone we knew was there; the church almost overflowed. Since we hadn't had a really meaningful conversation for a couple of months, today I felt an especially powerful urge to contact him.

Well, my love, today is your anniversary, so I thought I'd ask if there's anything special you want to share with me, or maybe you'd just like to tell me what's going on with you.

The most important thing for you to know is that I'm happier than I ever was in my body. I think I just never

gave myself permission to relax and enjoy myself. I was always waiting until everything was perfect to allow myself that luxury. And, of course, it never was.

In this dimension, joy is a natural state. That's not to say that every spirit is joyful all the time, but our value system is totally different. Your whole social structure is based on material success, which requires a daily struggle to achieve and compete and progress. There's no such thing where I am. Love and knowledge are the priorities, and they come from experiences of all kinds.

Can you explain how that works?

Well, the physical universe is like a school where we all put into practice the principles we've learned here when we're not in a physical body. And the earth is like a playground where we go to play games. It's a stage where we put on plays. It's a canvas where we paint pictures and a book where we write the stories we make up as we go along.

And all the sounds and sights and smells and tastes and feelings we experience there are part of the tapestry we weave when we're in a body. Then we come back here and take stock of all the things we did and felt and learned.

We usually take a rest to assimilate all of our lessons before deciding where we want to play next. It's all really play, you know, no matter how it feels. And it's all for our benefit and our growth process. **Whatever the experiences are, whether in the body or not, they're all valuable.**

Even the ones that involve suffering?

Absolutely. And the ones that involve pleasure, too.

Another thing you may not realize is that all of us here are learning from you at the same time you're learning from us. As you put your ideas into action in the physical world, we get to see how they work and how various principles are applied. Our perspectives may be different from yours, but we all work together for the benefit of the whole — or the Oneness.

Ah! So the learning goes back and forth and we're all playing student as well as teacher?

Always.

· · · · · ·

August 5, 1996

Today I needed to ask Bob some questions about parenting, since one of Terri's friends was having a rough time with her teenage daughter. I've always thought that being a parent was one of the toughest jobs in the world. And I've often wondered why no one teaches us how, except our own parents, who are all too often pretty sorry examples.

Could you give me some of your views on parenting this morning, Bob, especially about discipline?

You're right, being a good parent is very difficult and babies don't come with instruction manuals. One of these days they'll be teaching parenting classes in high school, but in the meantime, it's just trial and error.

One of the most important aspects of parenting is teaching children about cause and effect. Kids don't come into the world with a natural understanding of things like consequences. That's what parents are for, to show them where their actions will take them.

Adults have already learned the consequences of most of their actions. That is, you know where your behavior is likely to lead you, even though sometimes you close your eyes and pretend that planting poppy seeds will ultimately bring you roses.

In teaching cause and effect, the most crucial part, as well as the most difficult, is *consistency*. Unacceptable behavior on one day must be just as unacceptable the following day, even when you don't feel like taking the time and effort to enforce the rules.

You're right. I remember quite a few situations like that with my kids, especially when they were little. I knew I wasn't being consistent, but it wasn't always convenient to stop and discipline them.

Well, kids are smart; they play the odds. And if they can get by with something even half the time, it's worth a try. They could get lucky. But when they discover they can never get around your rules, they'll eventually stop trying. The point is, when they get out in the world and they're on their own, their mates, superiors, and law enforcement officers won't be as lenient and forgiving as their loving parents.

When it comes to teaching about consequences, consistency is vital, because the Universe is consistent. It doesn't make exceptions. When you pick up both feet, you will fall down. Always. And when you jump off a ten-story building, you'll get hurt. Always.

Hmmm....I see what you mean.

But children need to learn that consequences occur as a result of *all* actions—both positive and negative. And that these consequences don't always come from the source they might expect. Even if they don't get caught every time they lie or steal, there will still be consequences. By the same token, even if no one sees them doing a good deed, there will be positive consequences, too.

Children must also be taught that not only actions have consequences. Thoughts and words produce consequences, too. The energy behind thoughts and words operates exactly like a boomerang—whatever you put out inevitably comes back to you. It has to. That's the way the Universe works.

In other words, we need to teach our children the Golden Rule: "Do unto others as you would have others do unto you."

Correct. Ultimately you will get back everything you put out, but often in ways you couldn't possibly anticipate because they may appear unrelated. When you give out love, appreciation, generosity and encouragement, rest assured it will all come back to you with interest. But when you send out anger, hate and greed, all that negativity will boomerang right back in your face. And with interest, too.

Now the other side of discipline is praise. Because it's not enough to keep telling your children what they're doing wrong. You must let them know what they're doing right as well.

Haven't you noticed how your dancing teacher always points out what you're doing right? As a result, you've progressed much faster than you expected, and so has everyone else in the class. And it's all because of the way she teaches. She never makes you wrong.

Parents need to look for what's right and good and beautiful about their children, because when they do this, their children will instinctively repeat whatever has been praised.

That's precisely the way we function where I am, and that's what your guides do with you. You'll notice that everything that comes from your guides is basically positive. In fact, if it doesn't feel positive, it probably didn't come from them. It came from your own conscious mind.

But from a universal perspective, there's no such thing as "good" and "bad," is there?

No. There are no labels at all. But there are always two sides of the same energy—birth and death, spring and fall, winning and losing, joy and sorrow. And you learn and grow from all of it.

Do you remember watching your children trying to do something difficult when they were little and awkward?

Sure. They'd make all kinds of messes and botch everything up, but most of the time they'd keep right on trying until they succeeded.

Well, that's how we view humans on the earth plane. You're all doing the best you know how at your particular stage of development. We don't judge or criticize you any more than you would judge a child, knowing the limitations of his experience. And just as you expect different actions and results from your child at different ages or stages of development, we anticipate those same differences from you.

Someday, when you finally learn to allow that same latitude to your fellow human beings, the world will be a more harmonious place.

Thanks, Bob. I think I'll give this to Terri's friend to read. Maybe it will help.

℘ 18 ℘

The Importance of Personal Desire

September 20, 1996

Fourteen months after Bob's death I was beginning to long for a meaningful, loving relationship again. I wanted to share these feelings with Bob, just as I shared everything else with him, but this was a bit different than the other subjects we talked about and I felt embarrassed. And a little guilty, too. I didn't know if he expected me to remain alone and celibate for the rest of my life, or if he would feel hurt or jealous or what. But it was time to find out.

Honey, you know how much I miss you, but I'm starting to feel the need for some kind of a social life.

Okay.

What I mean is, I think I'm getting ready for a real live man again. You know, someone with a physical body.

I know what you mean.

So how do you feel about that? How do you feel about my having another man in my life? I really miss the romance.

I want you to be happy and fulfilled, my love. And if that's what will make you happy, I'm all for it.

Well, how would this work? Are you going to be hanging around watching me with someone else? I mean, it sounds a little kinky to me.

Don't worry. You'll have all the privacy you need.

Really? Or are you just saying that? You know, sometimes I wonder if you're with me all the time, even when I might not feel comfortable about it. Do you know what I mean, sort of like Big Brother watching me?

Yes, I understand. But that's not the way it works. I'm only with you when you want me to be, because it takes both of us to make the connection.

Oh, good. And you're sure you don't mind? You won't feel even the slightest twinge of jealousy?

No, honey. It's not like that here. We just want the best that life has to offer for our loved ones. And love in all its forms is the best that life has to offer. I'll even help you attract the kind of man you want. But it's up to you to decide what that is.

Great! Thank you.

You're welcome. Any time you have a heartfelt desire that's fueled by love and it doesn't hurt anyone or yourself, honor it. Desires are very healthy. They are the seeds that create your life.

Then why does religion always put down our desire nature?

Not all of them do.

Well, all those gurus and holy men in the East maintain that the most spiritual states occur when you rise above your desires. They sit around in their loincloths meditating all day and exist on practically nothing.

That is their desire.

I suppose you're right. So I guess there's really nothing wrong with desire.

Of course not. It's the key to everything in the universe. Desire is the seed of divine energy that gives birth to all movement, all progress, all growth—like the switch that starts an engine.

In the beginning, the desire of the Supreme Being created all life, and it's your personal desire that creates your individual life. Desire causes plants to reach for the sun, bees to make honey, humans and animals to crawl, run, learn, express, experience, have sex and multiply. Without desire, there would be no universe.

I never thought about it like that.

You see, before you came into physical form you decided on a general plan or path for your life. But once you're born into forgetfulness, how can you learn what that is? By listening to your desire nature. Your interests and passions lead you to your path and your purpose in life. So desires are not only a natural and healthy part of you, they're among your most valuable tools.

Your physical, mental, and emotional desires serve you constantly. It's obvious that physical desires such as eating, sleeping, having sex, and eliminating waste keep your bodies healthy. Desires for love, fun and pleasure nourish you emotionally and help keep your life in balance. Your natural curiosity and the desire for knowledge and experience keeps your mind active and constantly expanding.

As a rule, the more desire you have, the more zest for life and the more likely you are to fulfill your potential. A person with few desires sits back and lets life "happen" to him. Then when things don't work out, it never looks like his fault. He's an "innocent victim!" Total lack of desire is found in those who are physically, mentally or emotionally ill, or people who have given up and don't care any more.

This reminded me of my mother who went into a nursing home when she was around 80. For the first time in her life, she didn't want to hang up her favorite pictures or wear her own clothes or even have her personal things around her. She just didn't care any more, which was very unusual for her. She died about six weeks later.

Whatever you stop caring about or stop paying attention to will soon start to disintegrate, whether it's a house, a piece of clothing, your body, or your life. This is because the Universe assumes that whatever you pay attention to, you must want more of.

For example, if you're spending several hours a day cultivating your vegetable garden, you must want more vegetables. If you spend hours every day practicing the piano, you must want to be an accomplished pianist. On the other hand, if your days are spent in negative or destructive activities, you'll automatically attract more of the same.

If you'll remember, Bruce spent most of his time lying and stealing so he could buy drugs every day. He made friends with other drug addicts who also didn't work or go to school because they all thought the world owed them a living. So when he wound up in prison, he was surrounded by even more drug addicts. And now the state takes care of all of them.

So it doesn't matter what the object of our attention is, we'll always get more of it?

The Universe has no judgment about what sparks your interest, it merely responds automatically, like a fine-tuned machine. And the result is always predictable: whatever it is you're interested in *must* expand in your life. The formula is simple: time + energy + interest = desire. And desire = expansion.

It also doesn't matter whether your attention is directed outward on a physical level or inward on a mental or emotional level. It's all the same. For example, if you spend several hours a day worrying about your problems or plotting how to get even with someone you resent, the Universe interprets this to mean you want more problems and more things to resent. Therefore, prolonged worry will always create exactly what you don't want.

But we all worry sometimes, don't we?

Yes, and it's an enormous waste of time and energy. Think about it this way: if you can do something to resolve a problem, do it and you'll have nothing to worry about. If there's nothing you can do to resolve a problem, there's no need to worry about it.

Well, that's easier said than done.

True, but you must not turn your mind into a garbage dump. Your subconscious mind is your personal connection to the Universal Mind and registers *only* what you're picturing or imagining for yourself, not whether you really *want* that picture. The reason for this is that the subconscious doesn't understand the word "not." It simply deduces that what you're giving attention or energy to must be something you desire, so it automatically goes about creating more of it in your reality.

Therefore, your imagination must be used with great awareness and discrimination. Not only does it help you create incredible beauty, it can also provide you with vivid images of all the gruesome "what if's" that fill you with terror. And since these inner thoughts and emotions are the building blocks of your life, when you focus on worry, fear, and anger you simply attract more of the same.

I'm sure you've heard the saying, "You are what you eat." Well, it's true. However, what you ingest in *any*way becomes the raw material that creates your life and everything in it, including your physical body. In other words, what you take in, you give out. And what you give out, you receive.

Can you give me an example?

Of course. Look at the food you eat, specifically meat. At one time animals were raised on farms in a humane manner, with genuine concern for their needs. They served a family or community in whatever way was appropriate for them, and some ultimately gave their lives to feed their owners.

However, today animals are being raised by your industrialized society with no regard whatsoever for their comfort and well being. As a result, they live miserable, unnatural lives, full of rage, fear and hopelessness, that end in violence at the slaughterhouse.

In a country where the staples of your daily diets are hamburgers, steaks, ham, bacon and chicken, you are all ingesting this negative energy into your bodies every day. In other words, you are literally eating fear, rage, and violence. Since the environment of fish cannot be as rigidly controlled, they are far healthier for your bodies.

Is it any wonder that your society has become one of the most violent on earth? In the coming New Age, this situation will finally be acknowledged and remedied. In the meantime, however, remember that the food you eat is your basic fuel. So whatever that food is comprised of, is what you eventually become— physically, mentally, emotionally and spiritually. There's no way around it.

You also become what you see, hear, touch and smell—and whatever else you give your attention to. For example, a daily diet of violence and negativity from television, movies and newspapers eventually creates more of the same in your personal life.

It's like a cosmic mirror—what you notice you become. In other words, the energy you send out is mirrored back to you by the physical world and the result is called "your life."

That certainly places a lot of importance on what we choose to notice, doesn't it?

Absolutely, especially when everything in the universe is continually vying for your attention. And it's totally up to you to decide what to focus on. If you choose to spend your time and energy on people and activities you love, you will automatically attract joy and satisfaction as well as more love into your life.

On the other hand, if you choose to dwell on anger, frustration, worry, sadness, and whatever it is that seems to be missing in your life, guess what you're going to get more of? This isn't to say that these emotions are bad or even unnecessary, but they carry enormous power, which makes them a magnet for attracting more of the same.

If you concentrate solely on money and power, your marriage could fall apart out of sheer neglect. And if your home and family are claiming all your attention, your career ambitions could suffer. Balance is vitally important if you want to "have it all."

Take a look at your own priorities right now— meaning where you spend your time and energy—and you'll see exactly how they're manifesting in your life today. There's nothing "wrong" with anything you choose to focus on, of course, as long as you're aware of the consequences.

I was just thinking about my friend Phyllis who actually puts time aside for worrying every day. I guess that means she has to create a lot of stuff to worry about, although I'm sure she doesn't realize this consciously. I wonder what would happen if she spent the same amount of time every day doing something she loved?

For one thing, she'd be a lot happier. Just remember, whatever it is you want more of in your life, look for it, notice it, pay attention to it, appreciate it and express gratitude for it. But above all, *be it and give it* and it will expand. It has to. It's a Universal law.

For example, if you want more love in your life, open to all forms of love without limitation, conditions, and expectations. And don't assume it only looks or feels a certain way. Love takes many forms, so be ready to experience it in a variety of ways.

It's interesting that most people pray for someone to love them. They don't realize that the ultimate experience in life is to feel the love inside themselves and project it out to others. It's the feeling that is in your own heart that counts, not what is outside of you.

If you want more beauty in your life, look around and acknowledge every beautiful thing or person you see as you go through your day. Give thanks for everything beautiful that's already in your life. In your heart, thank the designer of a lovely dress you own or the architect of the magnificent building you work in or the Creator for a breathtaking sunset. Make it a habit to seek out beauty through sight, sound, smell, and touch everywhere you go. And make yourself beautiful, too, inside and out.

As you start noticing and looking for what you want more of, you'll soon find that your life is becoming packed to overflowing with it. Because whatever you devote your attention to will eventually fill your life. So it's up to you. You can focus on everything that's positive or everything that's negative. The more attention you give to what you're grateful to have, the more you'll have to be grateful for.

I was really fascinated with what Bob had to say, but I kept hoping he'd get back to the subject I started with—finding a new relationship. Eventually it was too late because I had to get dressed for an appointment. But I couldn't help wondering if he took off on that tangent to avoid talking about a new man in my life.

❧ 19 ☙

Bob's 12-Step Program
to Manifest Your Dreams

September 24, 1996

It still felt weird asking Bob to help me find a new romantic relationship, but since he'd become my guide, mentor and best friend, I decided what better person to ask? After all, he'd made it pretty clear that it wasn't like I was cheating on him. Besides, my horoscope was exceptionally favorable for attracting a new relationship in the next few months, and it looked like it would be with someone totally different from anyone I'd ever known.

Well, you said you'd help me attract a man into my life. Did you really mean that?

Of course.

Then I think I'm ready. What do I need to do? Are you going to give me some kind of a guideline?

How about a 12-step program? "12 Steps to Manifest Your Dreams." How does that sound?

Perfect!

First of all, understand that you are the physical counterpart of the Universal Consciousness, which is nonphysical. Together you are co-creators on the physical plane. You are the magnet that is constantly attracting experiences to you, which means that your whole life is the result of your desires.

I'm quite aware that most of the time it doesn't look that way. Part of the illusion has to do with *time*, since your desires usually take a certain amount of time to manifest. As a result, it's hard to understand that you are the cause and your life is the effect, especially when you've manifested something that feels negative. Somehow it never looks like your fault.

I guess we're just not used to noticing cause and effect. And change usually does seem to take forever.

Of course. But since there's no such thing as linear time where I am, desire and manifestation, occur simultaneously.

We keep sending you teachers and gurus to demonstrate that this is possible for you, too, but you refuse to believe their teachings. You insist upon worshiping these people instead of emulating them.

They perform what you call miracles, but a miracle is simply an immediate manifestation of desire. One of the primary differences between a "normal" event and a miracle is the *time* involved.

I never thought of it that way. You mean like Jesus instantly producing the loaves of bread and the fish to feed all the people?

Exactly. When you expect things to take time, they do. It all comes from your own mind. For example, when Terri was a teenager, how long did it take her to become a working actress?

About ten minutes. I took her to an agent and he signed her.

Right. Nobody told her that it was difficult to find an agent and get work, so she didn't expect it to be hard. And it wasn't. Now this may not be a typical example, but your beliefs and expectations often dictate how much time it takes to accomplish your desires.

Almost anything you can imagine is possible, but only if you're willing to do what it takes to make it a reality. Just be careful what you wish for, because you're playing with the most powerful energy in the Universe: desire plus imagination!

Step 1—DECIDE WHAT YOU WANT. You'd be surprised how many people know exactly what they *don't* want, but when it comes to what they *do* want, they haven't the faintest idea. They think they'll know it when they see it, but they never do. The idea must start in your own mind first.

Always state your desire in the present tense, as though it is true *now*, since the subconscious doesn't compute past or future. For example, if you ask to be physically healthy someday or to meet your ideal mate sometime in the future, you are literally asking to continue *wanting* these desires rather than actually *achieving* them. Therefore, you must affirm that your wish is already accomplished.

There is no power in the past or the future. You can enjoy memories of the past or the anticipation of future plans, but all you can thoroughly experience or control is the present.

Also, if your desire is vague, the response from the Universe will be vague, too. The more specific you are and the more committed to what you want, the more the Universe will be, too. Commitment is a powerful thing.

Step 2—WRITE DOWN YOUR DESIRE AND READ IT ALOUD. The spoken word has the greatest power because there's more energy and intention behind it than a thought or the written word. It's a physical expression, so when the mind hears the spoken word, it pays special attention and starts to believe what it hears. This is the power behind verbal affirmations.

They are even more powerful when spoken to another person and *most* powerful when spoken to a group of people. The same holds true for thoughts and words that come *from* a group. This is the reason behind repeating passages aloud or singing in church. The written word is next in power and after that is thought.

Step 3—ADD FEELING TO YOUR DESIRE. Feeling gives your desire the intensity it needs to manifest. The mental process is powerful, but it's too detached and analytical to produce results by itself. Your desire is made real to the degree of your passion, commitment and action. And the greatest fuel is emotion. It's like the electricity that makes your appliances work. For example, a TV set may *look* just fine, but it won't *do* anything until you plug it in.

Emotion is both the vehicle and the path to all new experiences and, therefore, is necessary to progress of any kind. Enthusiasm, love, passion and excitement are all powerful emotions, and the more you experience these feelings along with your words, the greater the result. The only thing that stops the process is fear.

Fear restrains and constricts. Much of what you call logic is really fear. You use logic to camouflage fear— both to yourself and to the world. You talk yourself out of what you really want by reasoning that it's too late, you're too old, there's too much competition, it will take too long, it's too expensive, and so forth.

Step 4—CLOSE YOUR EYES AND IMAGINE YOUR DESIRE A REALITY NOW. Feel it. See it. Visualize the end result already manifested and actually experience the feelings you expect to have when your desire is fulfilled.

Your imagination is the creative energy of the Universe which constantly works through you to form your future. When you imagine something, you are on your way to making it real. So always let your imagination go to the end result you want.

Step 5—ASK FOR "THIS OR SOMETHING BETTER" when you visualize what you want or when you pray to attract a specific person, job, or opportunity. Sometimes you don't know what's best for you in a particular situation, so don't try to second guess the Universe. You may know what's good, but you have no conception of what could be even better.

Step 6—TRUST THAT YOUR DESIRE WILL MANIFEST AND DON'T WORRY ABOUT HOW. Don't get attached to any particular way you think it *should* manifest. Be open to anything that's legal and doesn't hurt another person or yourself. You could be led to an entirely new path or adventure which is better than anything you could possibly have thought of yourself. So let the Universe figure out the strategy. Your positive, focused energy is enough to set in motion all the necessary steps to making your desire a reality.

Step 7—LET GO OF DESPERATION. Desperation impedes your progress and gums up the works by adding the element of anxiety, otherwise known as doubt. This is like having one foot on the gas and the other on the brake.

When you let go of conscious control and trust that everything will eventually work out to your benefit—

which it always does anyway—the Universe has more freedom to steer you toward your goal. If doubtful thoughts start interfering with your concentration, just accept them as a normal reaction from the logical mind and bring your focus back to your desire.

Step 8—TAKE ACTION TO DEMONSTRATE YOUR INTENTION. Intention backed up by action shows your willingness to do whatever it takes. This is part of your commitment or investment in your desire. You can't just huddle in a closet and expect the world to beat down your door. The combination of action and intention creates a powerful energy that never fails to attract the attention of the Universe. It's like the beacon from a lighthouse, and the Universe must respond to your desire. It has no choice.

Step 9—EXPECT THE BEST. Hold onto the memory of all the things that have worked out the way you wanted. Remember what you learned from past experiences when things didn't turn out the way you planned, but worked out better in the long run.

Step 10—TRUST THAT YOUR DESIRE WILL MANIFEST IN THE PERFECT TIME. Don't be discouraged if your desire takes longer than you expected. And if it doesn't work out at all, then it wasn't right for you, though you may not be able to see that until later. Or the timing may be off. Or maybe you haven't dreamed big enough. Or something better could be waiting just around the corner.

Step 11—BE GRATEFUL. Give thanks as you accept and acknowledge the results of your desires. The Universe wants you to enjoy your gifts and be happy. That's what life is all about.

Step 12—GIVE. Share the wealth, the joy, the knowledge and the passion with others. This expands it for you as well as everyone else. It will all come back to you like a boomerang. Share what you've gained, what you've accomplished, what you've created, what you've learned and what you've earned.

Pure giving is called charity, but you also share when you sell something you're proud of. So whether it's making clothes, growing tomatoes, singing a song or writing a book, send your treasures out into the world as you would your human children, to be loved and appreciated by others. Don't lock up your creations in a closet where no one can enjoy them. These are valuable expressions of you.

Thanks, Bob. This is really helpful. And I can see how these steps can be used for anything I want to manifest, not just a new relationship.

There's also a more condensed version called the Sacred Circle, which encapsulates the 12-Step Program. This is a powerful energy source consisting of four major points: DESIRE, RECEIVING, GRATITUDE, GIVING.

It makes no difference where you start, each of these points automatically leads you to the next one, because the energy of the circle is self generating. The more you use it, the more it recharges itself and creates its own momentum. Therefore, if you keep going around the circle you can manifest just about anything you want— all in its own perfect time, of course.

So how does it work?

When your desire becomes a reality, the next step is gratitude, which operates the same way in the Universe as it does in your personal life. For example, when a friend thanks you for a special kindness or your employer shows appreciation for the excellent work you do, you're naturally inspired to continue that behavior.

On the other hand, if someone keeps doing favors for you over a period of time and you never say thank you or express your gratitude in any way, that person will eventually stop doing those things. Well, the Universal Consciousness is no different. Your gratitude is important because it keeps the lines of communication open. Your appreciation for what you already have, as well as for what you've asked for and received, is a necessary part of the mix. It primes the pump, so to speak.

Well, that makes sense. Is that why we set aside a national holiday for giving thanks?

Believe it or not, that's part of what makes America so prosperous.

And what about giving?

It's important that whatever you give comes from the heart. When you give with resistance, you're not really helping anyone, including yourself. Give to those people and organizations you believe in. Give to causes you want to see expanded. In the overall scheme of things, the Universe doesn't care where or how you give, only that you do.

What about the street people who are always asking for handouts? Aren't most of them just going to buy more drugs with the money they get? How do we know if they really need it or not?

It's not up to you to determine whether someone is going to spend your donation on drugs or alcohol. That's not your problem. The act of giving is all that's important. And there are myriad ways to give besides money.

You can offer your time, love, talent, support, encouragement, advice, food, material things—all these are extremely valuable. But true giving is always what the other person wants or needs, not necessarily what's important to you.

This constant flow of giving, receiving and expressing gratitude emulates the basic nature of the Universe. Without that flow, life would eventually cease.

Thanks, Bob. Now I need to make a list of what I want in a man and get to work.

Good. We'll talk again when you decide what you want.

℘ 20 ℭ

What Your Relationships
Reveal About You

September 26, 1996

I began making a list of requirements for the new man I was looking for. However, since I wasn't interested in getting married or even living with someone at this point, the list turned out to be short and sweet. Most of all, I wanted an intelligent guy who was fun to be with and who shared at least some of my interests.

Okay, I think I've got my list together. I want a man who loves to dance, who's free to travel, and is terrific in bed.

That's it?

Well, yeah. I'm not looking for someone to be a husband or the father of my children or anything like that. So this should work out fine, don't you think?

This has nothing to do with me. It's your desire. I notice you're getting interested in sex again.

I was beginning to squirm a little, but I didn't back down.

Sure, why not. Isn't that okay?

Of course it's okay. In fact, it's very healthy. It will help keep you young.

Well, we'll see. I'm a little nervous about that, too. In fact, I'm nervous about the whole thing. You know, I must have an awful lot to learn about relationships in this lifetime, because I've had so many of them—three marriages and several "significant others!" I mean, that's quite a few, don't you think?

Some people need that many experiences—or even more. There's nothing wrong with having more than one partner. Life isn't the Cinderella story, you know. Just because you didn't meet the perfect person and stay married for your whole life doesn't mean you've failed or made a mistake. Relationships are simply experiences, like everything else. Some people have only one job during their lifetime and others have dozens. There's no right or wrong, or better or worse.

But why are relationships so difficult for most of us? It seems like the biggest problems we have to face involve relationships of one kind or another, and they're usually romantic ones.

Well, let's face it. I wasn't too good at relationships either, but I see things a lot differently now. You attract people into your life to give you the

opportunity to express who you are at that particular time. Relationships provide a vehicle for you to demonstrate your beliefs, feelings, desires and priorities.

For example, if you're going through a period where you're carrying around a lot of anger, you'll automatically magnetize someone into your life to whom you can direct that anger. If you're feeling inadequate or sorry for yourself, then those emotions will attract a person who gives you an opportunity to feel that way even more.

I've noticed that with my astrology clients—how they constantly attract people who allow them to play out the emotional state they were already in. I've seen it in my own life, too.

And you always will, because *you* are the magnet. The people and experiences that comprise your outer life are simply a mirror of what is going on inside of you. Therefore, since you always attract what you feel the need to express, everyone and everything in your life is constantly serving you.

And what about family members?

These are usually chosen for lifetime lessons, whereas short-term relationships indicate briefer ones. If you take a look at the people in your life right now, you'll see exactly what you've chosen to learn and express. In fact, you might want to make a list of those who are playing a major role and ask yourself these three questions about each one of them:

1. For what purpose have I attracted you into my life?

2. What are the lessons I've chosen to learn from our relationship?

3. What is the ultimate gift?

You might be surprised at how much you learn from this exercise, because your relationships provide a wealth of information about where you are in your life and how far you've progressed. The ones that give you the most joy always contain valuable lessons and rewards. But the most difficult relationships, those that provide your heaviest burdens and frustrations, are your greatest teachers.

Start with someone who stirs up the strongest feelings of anger, resentment or hurt, and who reacts the same way toward you. Now try to imagine how that person would react if you simply replaced all those negative feelings with love and understanding. In some cases, this may not be easy to imagine, but it's certainly possible.

Does that mean I have to approve of this person's behavior?

Absolutely not. But somewhere inside of him or her is a soul that longs for happiness and acceptance just as you do. So what do you think would happen if you dropped your judgments and your resistance? By changing *your* emotional climate, there would be no place for the other person's negative feelings to go. It's like playing ball with someone who's unwilling to receive the pass. The ball would just drop to the ground and roll away. The game is over.

So what you're really talking about is forgiveness, right?

That's correct. However, there seems to be a great deal of misunderstanding surrounding that word.

Forgiveness doesn't mean that you sanction a person's bad behavior or that what they've done doesn't matter. It's simply acknowledging that someone was playing a role in your life, that he or she was sent to help you learn something. And even though your experience was unpleasant, the relationship still served you and was probably the best thing that could have happened to you.

Forgiveness simply means letting go of the anger and resentment that binds you to the other person and replacing it with love and understanding, which frees you. When you let go of your resistance you are no longer playing the blame game.

Forgiveness allows you to fully tap into the full force of unconditional love, which is the greatest power there is. You can never "control" that power, but you can "log on" so that it's available to you—personally!

Too often you fall into the habit of judging the mistakes as the person. This includes self judgment, as well. It's not about the stumbling. It's about being there for yourself, no matter what. It's also about being there for others, no matter what. That's what taps you into unconditional love. Forgiveness is magic.

You say that we should drop our judgments about people, but how is that possible when they do terrible things that go against our principles?

Rather than judging people themselves, judge their behavior. Certainly it's important to know and express what is acceptable to you and what is not—in other words, what you stand for. In doing so you're defining yourself and your beliefs.

However, even when you disagree with someone's actions, never condemn their basic essence. Since you are all connected, you're simply condemning yourself. Honor the intrinsic goodness within each human being, and remember that you're all different forms of the same being or life force. The Universe has many forms and faces in order to play various roles on the stage of life.

As I look back on my own life and evaluate what I gained from my most difficult relationships, I see that these people deserve my deepest gratitude.

Why does it take us so long to learn these things?

It doesn't have to. It's up to you. You can draw out your lessons as long as you wish. You can keep repeating your experiences over and over for an entire lifetime, or for several lifetimes. But as soon as you acknowledge your part in attracting certain people into your life, your relationships will start shifting so they can help you progress instead of blocking you. Then you're ready to accept the gifts they bring.

෨ 21 ෬

Love & Sex:
The Life Force of the Universe

After I'd composed my list of what I wanted in a man, I embarked on Bob's 12-Step Program and followed it faithfully. I closed my eyes and meditated on my list of requirements every morning and affirmed that this person was already in my life. I imagined how I would feel around him and actually experienced those feelings as I visualized various scenes of us together. I imagined we were deeply in love and felt a strong physical attraction to each other. However, I didn't bother visualizing his face because I figured that as long as the chemistry was there, it didn't really matter what he looked like.

As it turned out, the man was already in my life. He had joined my metaphysical study group a few months earlier and we were just getting to know each other. His name was Jerry, and after one of our weekly meetings in July 1996, he gave me a newsletter about Tantra Yoga that contained an article he'd written. Now at that point, all I knew about Tantra was that it involved using sexual energy in spiritual ways, but the whole subject was really foreign to me.

When I read the newsletter the next day, I noticed an ad for a beginners Tantra workshop and felt an irresistible compulsion to sign up for it. I had absolutely no idea why, but I decided it must have something to do with the special breathing technique they taught.

My friends were horrified. They couldn't imagine being so adventurous themselves, and I could tell that a few of them had serious doubts about my sanity. One of them even remarked, "You'll probably be the same age as their mothers!" But I felt I had no choice....I was destined to go to this workshop.

My friend was right, of course. When I showed up for the weekend, almost everyone there was young enough to be my child—and in some cases my grandchild—but it didn't really bother me. I was surprised to see Jerry there, since it was for beginners, and he was even more surprised to see me.

I must admit that I'd always felt attracted to him, but since he was obviously much younger, I ignored the feeling. As I watched him interact with women his own age that weekend, I just admired him from across the room. The Tantra workshop was the first time we'd seen each other outside my study group, and sharing that experience was the beginning of a genuine friendship between us.

About the same time I began Bob's 12-Step Program, Jerry asked me to do his horoscope and I learned a lot more about him. Not only was he 19 years younger than I, but his background couldn't have been more different. His parents had miraculously survived the Holocaust and he was born in a refugee camp in Germany right after the war. He grew up in Brooklyn, was married once, had no children, and had lived in Israel for several years. He'd been an actor, artist, writer and TV producer and was currently writing a book about sex that he felt was his life's work.

I could see from his horoscope that he would soon find out what real love was all about and that it would totally change his life. So I told him he was getting ready to experience the greatest love he'd ever known and that he would never be the same again. I swear I had no idea it was *me*!

Having shared the workshop and the intimate details of his horoscope, Jerry and I began going out occasionally...as friends. Since he loved to dance, I invited him to join me for a ballroom dancing class and we had a lot of fun. We also met for lunch a couple of times...strictly as friends, of course. After all, we were from two different generations.

One day in early November Jerry came over to borrow a book, and in a single instant both of our lives were transformed forever. As we walked into my living room, he reached for my hand and said, "I'm in love with you." Since we'd never kissed or even held hands before, I was understandably a bit flabbergasted!

"But, Jerry, I'm a lot older than you!"

He just grinned. "So?"

At that moment, I realized this was the man I'd been dreaming of. And as it turned out, he was far more than I had asked for or could even imagine. Not only did he love to dance, he was a writer who could travel whenever he pleased. And it didn't take long to discover he was also the most amazing lover I'd ever had. On top of that, he was brilliant, sensitive, generous, creative and was drawn to all the metaphysical subjects that fascinated me. How lucky can you get?

However, at that point, I didn't have a clue about the *real* reason we were together. I had no idea that eventually we'd discover there was a far more compelling purpose to our relationship than just having a good time.

. . . . . .

November 23, 1996

Swept up in my new love affair, I hadn't communicated with Bob for a couple of weeks. This morning as I picked up my pen, I felt myself glowing—I was in love.

Good morning! Can you see how happy I am?

Of course. I see you manifested your desire very quickly! I also notice that it didn't look exactly the way you pictured it. But you opened your heart anyway, and I commend you for that. You'll be glad you did.

You're right. I would never have imagined a relationship with someone 19 years younger than I am! In fact, I'm still in shock. Is this really going to work?

Why not? Jerry will be very good for you. Besides, I don't recall anything on your list about age. You got everything you asked for and a lot more with all your interests and beliefs in common. Besides, he'll keep you young.

For a while maybe. But he's such a fantastic guy, he could have some gorgeous woman closer to his own age any time he wanted. I'm terrified that he'll wake up some morning and suddenly realize this relationship is totally insane.

You know, of course, that you're simply wrestling with your own judgments.

I'm just trying to be realistic. Is there something wrong with having judgments?

Absolutely not. You need judgments to function in your reality because, along with your beliefs, they help you make choices and decisions. But understand that there's no reality involved in a judgment. You're just putting your own label on something.

And from a universal perspective, there are no labels.

I see you've been listening.

Well anyway, it feels glorious to be in love.

You're always "in love."

What do you mean?

You can never be "out of love." Love is the life force.

Oh, right.

Get used to the idea that love and the life force are one and the same thing. There can never be a lack of love in the Universe, although there may be a lack of relationships or activities through which you can express your love.

So are you saying that we human beings are made of love? Somehow that's hard to grasp.

I understand, but it's true. Every living thing in the Universe is the embodiment of God's love. You are the manifestation of love in physical form. In fact, you have created your body in order to express your love in the physical world.

Your body is a direct reflection of who you are and what you've learned. And as an energy field, you attract people and experiences into your life according to your vibration through the law of magnetic attraction. Every thought you have is literally converted into matter by your spirit.

You express your love through everything that attracts you, but primarily through relationships and creativity. You express it through the arts, through your appreciation of beauty and by collecting things you admire. The energy of love can even be felt from the inanimate objects you treasure, which actually reflect your love back to you in your home.

Love is your most valuable contribution to the Universe. As a matter of fact, that's all the Universe asks of you—to express your love in as many ways as possible—through work, relationships, creativity, children, family, and all your favorite activities.

The more love you feel and give freely and unconditionally, the more love you attract into your own life and the more you have to give out again. In perpetuating this circle, you are nourishing the entire Universe, as well as yourself.

Love nourishes like no food ever can. It stimulates you, motivates you, and adds the passion to life that gives you a reason to live. It promotes good health, longevity and joy, and is the greatest medicine known to mankind.

In fact, medical science has finally proven that love has healing powers far beyond the scope of our doctors and their technology. When I was in the hospital in 1989, trying to decide whether to stay or leave, it was your love, Joy, that kept me in my body.

That's amazing! And when Jackie had her near death experience in Egypt, the main thing that convinced her to stay was the love of her children and all the people who were praying for her at the time.

Science has found nothing more powerful than the life force itself. And it never will. It's the energy that allows a blade of grass to break through a concrete sidewalk.

The life force is composed of pure love. And in relationships, pure love has no expectations—it's unconditional and complete in itself. You don't love your children on the condition that they love you back. You just feel it in your heart and let it pour out. When you give love from your heart, it's impossible not to

get it back. It may not come from the person you gave it to, but it must return to you from someone or somewhere.

Artists experience this purity when they pour love into their creations...and great art is often the result. By doing what you love the most, your own greatness is revealed. Therefore, always go where the love is, because that's where you'll find your highest power. If you do this, you'll never have to worry about whether you're on the "right path." Because when you surround yourself with the people, things and activities you love most, you are fulfilling your highest purpose on earth.

. . . . . .

January 3, 1997

During the last few years of our marriage, my sex drive had dwindled down to almost zero. I'm afraid that Bob wasn't the most creative guy in the bedroom and I was getting bored with the lack of variety. I actually felt relieved when he finally began to slow down in that department. After he left, I wondered if I would ever feel sexy again, but when Jerry came along, that problem changed overnight.

I can hardly believe it, honey! I feel like I'm 30 years old again — like my sex drive never left me!

Well, let's be honest. I knew you were getting bored with our sex life, even though I thought it was the best I'd ever had. But then, everything is relative. For you, it was never quite as imaginative and romantic as you wanted.

You're right, but at that point in my life I didn't think it really mattered very much.

Well, I see you've changed your mind, because now you have everything you ever dreamed of—and more than you thought possible.

I know. But, honey, I was never unhappy about our situation. I loved you so much that our sex life—or lack of it—was never any threat to our relationship. I felt that you were the one who missed it.

I did, but when I looked back and reviewed my life, I discovered that the reason I lost my sex drive was to force me to learn about intimacy in other ways. I had only experienced intimacy on a physical level and I thought that was all there was to it. Both of us had enjoyed a lot of sex in our lives, but our next lesson was about mental and emotional intimacy.

It was a good thing you lost your sex drive earlier than I did, though, so I didn't feel quite so lousy when mine started to wane. If you'd still been going strong, I would have felt like I was letting you down. As it was, it worked out perfectly and we finally did become more intimate on an emotional level.

That's true. And I can see how that was necessary for both of us. I learned to be more honest with you about my feelings, and yet I know there were times when I still held back.

You will learn even more about this with Jerry. Intimacy is about telling the truth—first being honest with yourself and then sharing that with others. It's about letting down the barriers you normally hide behind because you think no one will approve of you if they really knew you. Intimacy is the ultimate connection with other humans. It is what only feels safe between you and God.

Thanks. I see I have more to learn. Now I have another question for you, which may sound a little strange, but do you have sex where you are?

Not as you know it, but in other ways. It's something like the intensely loving *feelings* you experience when you're having passionate sex. Now multiply that ten times. It's not a physical orgasm like you have—it's more like what you'd call an emotional orgasm.

What do you mean by that?

It's hard to describe, but we become so full of love that there comes a point where it feels like we're exploding. I think it's even better than a physical orgasm, although some spirits don't agree.

How do you feel about sex now from where you are?

I see a lot of things differently from this perspective, and sex is one of them. If love is the life force of the Universe, sex is the heartbeat. Sex is what love *does*.

It's the movement or pulse of love. It's the constant creation of new life, the cosmic generator that keeps everything humming. When two people "make love," that's literally what they're doing. They're actually creating love and sending it out as a gift to the Universe.

Various societies and civilizations have had many different belief systems over the centuries regarding love and sex...and still do. Not that any of them are right or wrong, they are simply choices made by each group to fit their particular needs. For example, the basic structure of the society determines whether monogamy or polygamy is suitable or acceptable and this is simply a matter of agreement.

So there are no universal rules and regulations about sex, like limitations on the number of people we should be having sex with, or the gender?

No. Many civilizations have sanctioned homosexuality as a perfectly natural and acceptable expression of love, and many encourage multiple partners. It is humans who put labels and limitations on sex through their religions and belief systems, the same as they do on everything else. But these are not universal labels. As I've said before, there *are* no universal labels.

Sex is one of the highest expressions of Universal Love. It is the energy of creation. But all energy must include its opposite, and the opposite of creation is destruction. Don't you think it's curious that your society constantly presents every possible form of destruction and violence through your various media, while doing everything in its power to hide the beauty and ecstasy of sexuality?

Yes. I always felt that was backwards somehow.

You will start to see this pattern shift within your lifetime.

Good. And by the way, I want to know how you really feel about my having a sexual relationship with someone else?

Honey, I think it's great. I also notice that Jerry is keeping you young, just as I predicted. You know, it's quite amazing to be able to perceive your joy as you go through life. When I was there, I never knew that anyone could be as happy as you. I certainly wasn't! I was always worrying about something. I was so afraid there wouldn't be enough time or money or health or sex, or whatever I thought was necessary to make me happy. Actually, there was always enough, and I still wasn't happy. What a waste!

℘ 22 ℘

Bob's Most Important Lesson

January 8, 1997

Today was Bob's birthday—the second since he passed on—and I remembered how I'd planned on throwing him a big party for his 70th birthday last year...but by then he was gone. He probably wouldn't have liked it anyway, since big parties never appealed to him that much. He'd rather have a few friends over for dinner and poker.

Bob had never been the type to celebrate his own birthday, but that changed after we were married. Probably because of the special evening I arranged for him on every birthday...except his last.

When he came home from work, I'd meet him at the door in my sexiest lingerie—garter belt, black stockings, spike heels, the works—and a glass of champagne. Then I'd undress him and usher him into a hot bubble bath, followed by a relaxing massage and a nap. When he awoke refreshed, we'd drink more champagne and I'd serve his favorite dinner by candlelight. Of course, I was the dessert, which included all his favorite treats, if you know what I mean.

Happy Birthday, my love! I have a special question for you this morning. What do you feel is the most significant thing you've learned since you left your body that might be helpful to those of us who are still here?

That's a big question! But the answer would probably be this: *Everything that happens in your life is ultimately for your benefit.*

Obviously, it's hard to see this when you're in the throes of a trauma, but after the storm subsides, you'll always find the rainbow if you look for it.

I put down my pen and took a moment to think about what Bob said. Looking back on my life, several events came to mind that seemed negative at the time, but ultimately turned out to be for my benefit.

Back in the sixties I had a job I hated because my boss was a tyrant, but I was hesitant to leave because we needed my paycheck to make ends meet. Then all of a sudden I got fired for the first time in my life and I was devastated — how were we going to pay our bills? But the very next day I landed one of the best jobs I'd ever had.

I remembered another incident during my first marriage when the bank turned down my application for a loan to pay off my husband's debts. I was depressed for a week. But as it turned out, not getting the loan was the best thing that could have happened, because *I* would have been the one stuck with all the payments after the divorce.

Then I got to thinking about the really horrible things people go through and I started to wonder what Bob would say about that.

Well, that's a beautiful concept, but it's a little hard to swallow whole...without exceptions, that is. I can see where a lot of experiences could turn out to be blessings in disguise, but what about someone's house burning down? Or being raped or mugged or losing your life savings? Wouldn't it be awfully hard to find the rainbows in situations like that?

Initially, yes. But looking back from a different perspective, the reasons will always be clear to you if you search for them. As I said, you may not understand the true significance of each situation while it's happening, and that's not what you need at that point anyway. But a firm belief in this law will help pull you through all the traumas and tragedies of your life.

You might find it interesting to examine some of the experiences in your own life that seemed unbearable at the time and determine what the ultimate benefit was. For example, take a look at what it took to open your heart and acknowledge your own feelings.

You're right. It took the death of my brother and two children just to crack me open — and even after that I had a long way to go. I just didn't want to deal with my feelings. I thought they weren't important — that they didn't matter.

Well, guess what...feelings are what matter the most. We both had a lot to learn in this area, which is why we were together. It's important to learn to control and direct your feelings, but first they have to be acknowledged and experienced internally. And we both went too far in denying them.

I wish I'd understood more about the importance of feelings earlier in my life so I wouldn't have had to create so much trauma.

Trauma and suffering are both opportunities for growth—and that's exactly what you needed to break through your emotional barriers. Can you see how the loss of your brother and children helped you along your path? They were your greatest teachers.

I guess I never thought about it that way before. Without the challenge of having to cope with those losses, I would probably have remained superficial for the rest of my life. And that's not the kind of person I wanted to be. Looking back, I can see that I needed to experience those tragedies to realize the depth of who I was.

Tragedy is always a blessing in disguise, although it's not easy to see it at the time.

So what about you, Bob?

That's easy, the murder gave me a whole new life. It was the catalyst that brought me love in many forms—with you, Terri and Elliot, and finally, an honest, intimate relationship with Bruce.

I see now that Bruce came into my life to open my heart. Do you have any idea what it's like to have the son you adore incarcerated and ostracized by the whole world? You can't possibly imagine the agony! But it's exactly what I needed to break through my emotional barriers.

The father role was an important step for me because it taught me unconditional love. I finally learned to put someone else's needs ahead of my own—and it actually felt good. For the first time, I gave without any thought of receiving. And that relationship helped prepare me for you.

During my marriage to Dorka, I learned what happens when you force your will on others. She never wanted Bruce to begin with, but I insisted. As a result I had to deal with her resistance for 17 years and finally, with the tragic consequences of my own selfishness. Not that the Universe judges any of it as good or bad. That's obviously what I needed to learn about cause and effect.

Of course, now I know that every experience of our life leads us to the next step in our progress, because when one door closes, another one always opens. It doesn't matter what the situation is—win or lose, success or failure—there's always a gift, it is always positive and in the long run, the outcome will always be for our personal benefit.

So you're saying that there are no exceptions to this law, even when it comes to things like death and suffering?

That's correct. There are no exceptions. And my life is a prime example, as I've just described it. I realize that it takes a lot of faith to believe that everything happens for our benefit, because every new dilemma

always appears so different from previous ones. But rest assured, this law will keep working in the future without exception, just the same as it has in the past. Universal laws don't change.

You know, when I stop to think about it, we wouldn't even be having these conversations if you were still in your physical body...which is another example of a new door opening because another one closed. It reminds me of the first words you said to me on my way to the hospital the day you left. Do you remember?

Of course. I said, "I figured I could help you more from over here than from there." Now maybe you can understand what I meant.

Yes, I think I do. At first I thought you were talking about removing the burden of your illness from me by letting go of your own life. And then I thought maybe you were referring to setting me up financially so I wouldn't have to worry. But now I realize it was about the opportunity to write this book, which has been one of the most incredibly fulfilling experiences of my life.

I want to thank you again, my love, for all your wisdom and insight, for listening to me when I was down, for guiding me through a very difficult time, and finally for helping to bring even more love into my life. Good night, sweetheart, and God bless you.

· · · · · ·

Dear Reader, I hope you will use the meditation process I've described in Chapter Four to contact your own loved ones and guides. Believe me, it is definitely worth the effort. There are hundreds of methods and techniques for meditation, and all of them are effective. I encourage you to experiment with a few until you find the one that works best for you. Just make sure you use the energy of love as your pathway.

Once the connection is made, you'll find a whole new dimension has been added to your life. You can continue to enjoy the rewards of a loving relationship with anyone who has passed on by plugging into the Source of All That Is — the Energy of Love. And now that science has proven that energy can't be destroyed, we know that love never dies...and neither will you!

⁊ *Epilogue* ᚲ

As I began an exciting new chapter in my life with my new love, my conversations with Bob became less frequent, but sometimes we still talk while I'm in the shower, taking walks or driving the car. Whenever I tune into his vibration, he's right there for me as always—my Rock of Gibraltar.

Bruce is 34 years old now and has served more than 17 years in prison. An expert computer programmer, he participates in numerous rehabilitation programs and has become a trusted liaison between the guards and inmates. I'm extremely proud of the man he is today, and although I still don't know the truth about his guilt or innocence, at this point it is totally irrelevant to me. When he's finally set free, I will do everything in my power to see that he gets a chance to create a new life for himself.

Jerry and I have been together for three and a half years now and are still enjoying the most romantic relationship of our lives. In the past three years we've traveled to Cancun, New Orleans, Atlanta, Miami, Maui, Sedona, Carmel and Las Vegas, attended Tantra workshops, snorkeled nude in the Caribbean, attended rock concerts, and become enthusiastic swing and salsa dancers. We've made love on the beach of a fishing village in the Yucatan, on a swinging bed in the oldest

Bed & Breakfast west of the Rockies, in the hammock on my patio by moonlight, and in bubble baths by candlelight. Talk about romantic!

And just as Bob said, I'm learning more about intimacy than I've ever experienced before. Jerry and I accept each other exactly as we are and make it safe to share our feelings. Not that we don't run into emotional snags once in awhile, but we welcome that as part of the process of learning how to open up and become vulnerable with each other.

The most extraordinary part of our relationship, however, is something that took us awhile to discover. First Jerry began helping me organize this book, which would never have gotten out into the world without his encouragement and advice. And I began to help edit his novel, "The Secret Sex Life of Angels," in which he presents a remarkable new vision that could ultimately transform the way the world thinks about sex and spirit.

In the process of working together, I've discovered a whole new level to our relationship and a purpose far greater than I ever dreamed of. One day as I was editing a chapter of Jerry's novel, I was surprised when Bob started speaking to me, and I quickly wrote down his words.

Don't think you're doing this work just for Jerry. It's for you too, you know. This opportunity has come into your life as a result of your own attitudes about the way sex is censored, while violence is given free reign. These feelings have been intense enough to attract a project of this kind.

We are pleased that the two of you are working together and we are excited about what Jerry is saying. The message is important and it is time for the world

to hear it. You would never have done this alone and Jerry would be having a much more difficult time writing his book without you.

This book is the primary reason you were attracted to each other. Therefore, you are not doing Jerry a favor, you are doing this for yourself and for the world. The reason you're enjoying your involvement so much is that it touches a deep part of your soul.

When Bob passed on, I thought my world was coming to an end. How could I possibly have imagined that, with his help, I'd build a new life, find a new love and devote myself to shining a new light on two of the most misunderstood areas of our lives—sex and death. And I know from the depths of my soul that Bob's love will be there to guide me every step of the way.

෨ *Afterword* ෪

"The Joyful Redemption"
by I. Jerry Weinstock

Dear Reader,

It's 2010—ten years since **Love Ever After** was originally published. On the occasion of this 10th anniversary edition, I want to update you on Joy's extraordinary life (she "graduated" in 2007) and the miraculous events that have transpired in the last ten years.

Joy and I were madly in love. Friends described us as "magic." And why not? We were literally a "match-made-in-heaven." From the moment we fell in love, I spent almost every night at Joy's place and used my home as an office. In 2000, after three years of being together, I sold my townhouse and moved into Joy's condo. In 2002, we were married on a black lava beach in Hawaii surrounded by family and a few close friends. Then we swam with the dolphins.

To help others find the love of *their* dreams, we decided to share Bob's 12-Step program and created a workshop called **12-Steps to Findng Your Soulmate** that we taught at the Learning Annex and elsewhere. These workshops inspired several matches that have lasted to this day.

Our explorations into sacred sexuality continued both privately and professionally. Joy wrote about her renewed sex life in an essay entitled, *Sexy at Seventy,* that was published in "Our Turn, Our Time"—a book celebrating the second half of women's lives. Of the thirty contributors selected from a nationwide writing contest, Joy's essay was the only one about sex. Even when visiting Bruce in prison we always stayed in a room at the nearby Sutter Creek Inn that had a swinging bed.

Bob was a continual presence in our life. Joy didn't talk to him every day the way she had initially, but he was there for her whenever she needed guidance. The smell of cigarettes in our condo signaled his presence. "Bob's here," Joy would say delighted with a visit. Then she'd sit quietly, close her eyes and go within to hear whatever message he had for her.

Film producers, interested in developing a movie based on *Love Ever After* and our strange "threesome," wondered if it bothered me that Joy was still talking to her late husband. On the contrary, I thought it was fantastic.

After *Love Ever After* was published, Joy gave readings at various bookstores around LA, including several Barnes & Nobles and the famous spiritual bookstore, The Bodhi Tree. She was also interviewed on the radio and shared Bob's wisdom with listeners of The Aware Show on KPFK.

Life was great! We were traveling, writing my book, promoting Joy's book, giving workshops, making love... when on Mother's Day 2001 we discovered a lump in Joy's breast! Our four year honeymoon was over.

On a Friday afternoon Joy received the dreaded phone call from her doctor—she had breast cancer. Despite the terrible news, she led a workshop the very next day on Bob's "12 Steps to Manifest Your Dreams."

Naturally, Joy turned to Bob for guidance about how to deal with the cancer. He told her to cut sugar out of her diet and encouraged her to do research until she found a path that resonated with her because her belief was a powerful factor in her healing.

Bob said he couldn't and wouldn't make the decision for me, that the energy and enthusiasm behind my decision was a big part of what would make it work. And I would have to come to that myself.

Bob urged Joy to view her cancer as "an adventure" which would ultimately make her healthier and from which she would learn many lessons and receive many gifts. And that's exactly what happened.

We ate healthier, mostly organic. We juiced and I grew sprouts. Joy mixed traditional and alternative approaches to cancer. For example, we'd learned that laughter was important in strengthening the immune system. So every evening we had our dinner watching two comedies—*Cheers* and *Seinfeld*. When Joy was wheeled into surgery for her mastectomy, she was laughing hysterically to a comedy album. The nurses said they'd never seen anything like it. After a weekly chemo shot in the morning, we went dancing in the evening. I don't want to diminish the challenge that cancer was for Joy but she chose to look for the gifts and so she found them.

Joy often said that cancer was relatively easy in comparison to losing most of her sight and becoming "legally blind" from macular degeneration in the space of a few months during the late summer and fall of 2002. At my urging, she kept a tape recorded journal of that year's ordeal which she ultimately called, "Vision Quest."

Strangely the cancer never frightened me like this. I never thought it was fatal and always felt I could cure it, but going blind was something else entirely. It was appalling how quickly my vision deteriorated in just 10 days. I felt that the condition was totally out of my control and there was nothing I could do to stop it.

Initially, she was devastated. Fiercely independent, she could no longer drive, read or write. Thankfully, she still had her peripheral vision so she could walk around.

It was extremely difficult to apply makeup or even comb my hair...I cried with feelings of anger and hopelessness I hadn't experienced before. I felt old and tired and worn out...dependent, helpless. I sobbed in Jerry's arms for hours while he held and consoled me the best he could. No more playing bridge, no more reading, no more driving, no more independence of any kind as far as I could see. Without my sight there was no point in doing a lot of things I'd been looking forward to. The quality of my life looked so bleak to me that I even wondered if I wanted to go on living.

In her inimitable way and with her indomitable spirit (and, of course, with Bob's guidance) Joy gradually found the gifts in her sudden blindness.

Bob told me that the divine purpose of the macular degeneration was to develop my inner vision...that I would eventually be able to see things that others don't see...and that I would become a seer. This gift will be revealed to me at the right time.

Joy's year of going blind was one of the most difficult passages of her life. Yet ultimately, with Bob's guidance and my support, she declared during a 2nd appearance on The Aware Show in 2005 that "I've lost my sight but gained my vision."

To share Joy's psychic gift we created a monthly event called the *Sunday of Joy* where for several years she gave people psychic readings and answered their most pressing questions. Here's an example of the impact she had on people's lives, from a man who was dragged by his wife to a Sunday of Joy.

"I must admit I was skeptical, but as I listened to Joy speak I knew she was special. So I asked a question about the future of my company. She said that there would be some upheaval and that my staff would change due to major difficulties, but in the end I'd come out ahead and the company would thrive.

I was stunned, but I had a gut feeling that something was going on with my bookkeeper. That week I hired an outside expert to review my books who discovered that $100,000 had been embezzled. When my bookkeeper was investigated by the police, she admitted the crime and was arrested.

Two weeks later I discovered that two other employees were trying to undermine my company. So I fired them. I didn't think I could survive without them. But I hired new employees and now we're doing great! So what Joy predicted came to be!"

Though our honeymoon was over after four years and we dealt with cancer and blindness for the next six years, we were continually amazed at how wonderful our life was. Incredibly, despite all Joy's health challenges, our love grew and our intimacy deepened. Joy deserves most of the credit for making our life together wonderful because she always focused on the "gifts."

Gifts of cancer? Joy claimed that having cancer taught her to put herself first. Until then everyone else came first. She often said that the "gift" of her blindness was that she had to learn to *receive*. She'd been the *giver* all her life, but now she was dependent on others and had to learn how important the receiver was in the dance of life. To her this was a gift because it made her grow.

Blindness not only opened Joy's "inner vision," but she claimed it put her more in touch with herself. Unable to see people's faces or read the expression in their eyes, freed her from having to take care of them...or caring what they thought. She became more direct and expressed herself with a freedom she'd never experienced before.

Joy was awe-inspiring. She always chose happiness. Always looked on the bright side of life. And (almost) never felt like a victim. When people asked if she was angry about what had happened, Joy said No. She felt that cancer and blindness challenged her to *walk her talk*. And boy did she.

Despite these two health challenges, each of which would have devastated most people, Joy was still the happiest person you've ever met. Her secret? She looked for the gift in everything. She took Bob's teaching to heart—*Everything happens for your ultimate benefit.*

Despite our plans for my novel about sexuality (which we'd learned from Bob was one of the reasons we'd come together), we became increasingly preoccupied with Joy's cancer and blindness. In the midst of life-threatening challenges, my book seemed unimportant. Even so, I continued writing whenever I could and Joy continued editing. Even when she could no longer see, she had me read new pages to her line by line. It was painfully slow going but she loved doing it. Knowing that our time together was limited, I didn't have the heart to isolate myself to write, but instead focused my energies on healing her cancer and making her life as fulfilling as possible. And I never completed *The Secret Sex Life of Angels.*

. . . . . .

Bruce was a constant in our life. We visited him in prison and spoke to him on the phone almost daily. When Joy lost her vision I took over many of the practical details of handling Bruce's affairs—prepping quarterly packages for him, ordering books and magazines, buying clothes and even eyeglasses, as well as overseeing the building of his website.

Bob kept assuring us that one day Bruce would be free. Though Joy asked Bob if Bruce was guilty or innocent, Bob wouldn't answer, saying the truth would come out at the appropriate time.

It didn't matter to Joy whether Bruce was guilty or innocent because she'd grown to respect and love him. As I got to know Bruce over the years, I grew to respect and love him, too. Despite the horror and brutality he'd experienced, he was neither bitter nor cynical. Despite being "buried alive" he remained optimistic and hopeful that one day the truth of his innocence would be revealed and he would be free. However, as the years passed and every legal attempt to reopen his case was thwarted, it seemed that he was going to rot in prison for the rest of his life.

And then something incredible happened. The homicide detective responsible for Bruce's conviction so many years earlier wrote an unsolicited letter to the parole board that regularly reviewed Bruce's case. The letter claimed that the detective had recently visited the Lisker home where the murder took place and discovered that the new owners had found some missing money, evidence that corroborated the prosecution's case.

When Bruce told us about the letter to the parole board and that he was filing a complaint with the LAPD because the letter was a complete fabrication, Joy and I recognized the "hand of destiny." Like some mythic villain who overreaches, the man responsible for putting Bruce in prison, in his attempt years later to hammer the final nail in Bruce's coffin, was ironically going to become Bruce's savior. We didn't know how Bruce would regain his freedom but we could see the writing on the wall. And now we had no doubt—Bruce was innocent.

Bruce's complaint forced the LAPD to open an Internal Affairs investigation. The officer assigned to Bruce's case conducted a year-long investigation during which he not only discovered that the detective's letter was a complete lie—he'd never even been to the Lisker house, let alone talked to the new owners—he also discovered exculpatory evidence that would have proved Bruce innocent but had been withheld at Bruce's trial, most importantly a bloody shoe print of an intruder that corroborated Bruce's testimony.

The Internal Affairs officer recommended that Bruce's case be reopened due to his likely innocence. His superiors, however, told him to shut his investigation down because "that @#!% is staying in prison." The *LA Times* got wind of the cover-up and conducted their own exhaustive six month investigation which they published in an explosive front page story in the Sunday edition.

"A CASE OF DOUBT: New Light On A Distant Verdict" by staff writers Scott Glover and Matt Lait presented Bruce's case and the way it was mishandled 22 years ago. They practically re-tried the case. The prosecutor, who convinced a jury of Bruce's guilt so many years ago, was quoted as saying, "I now have reasonable doubt."

The day the *LA Times* article appeared (May 22, 2005), Joy recorded her feelings on tape in a voice choked with emotion.

Bob's been with me all morning. And he's crying! And I'm crying! We've been waiting for this day for 22 years! It's been a long time coming.

Bob said he's been working very hard on the Other Side to accomplish what's happening now. He cared the most, so he's been spearheading it. But he had a lot of help. And he also said that when he was here in this reality he wanted to do something very important as an attorney. And he never felt that he did. And the last thing he expected was that it would come through his son Bruce who was such a problem and such a heartache for him.

And as it turned out, this was the opportunity to do something important and to help change some laws that had to do with the Statute of Limitations for people who were innocent of the crimes they were arrested and incarcerated for. Twenty two years is a long time. And it's going to make news. And it's going to change laws.

And when I said to Bob, "I'm so happy that you're finally going to right this wrong." He said, "It's only wrong on a very small scale. It's 'wrong' because of our perspective here and it gives us the opportunity to turn it around. But on a very broad scale it wasn't 'wrong' at all. You have to pull back a long way to get the perspective to see that there are no 'wrongs' and that everything is perfect. Bruce is doing what he came here to do." And so did Bob. And so am I. And so are all of us.

So Bob and I are very emotional this morning. Because he left Bruce in my charge and he was telling me how proud he is of Bruce and me, and how much he appreciates my help just hanging in there with him. That's all I needed to do. Just be there for him and believe in him and help him.

And especially hanging in there when I really didn't know what the truth was. But I knew Bruce was trying and I knew he was worthwhile and I knew that was my job. It took a while to make sure of what the truth was. So that's why I had to find out for myself instead of being told a long time ago.

Bob has been gone almost 10 years. So it's taken a long time, plus the 12 years while he was here in a body. And he's telling me how frustrating it was for him and how heartbreaking it was. Literally. *Heartbreaking!* But it's all okay because that's what he chose and that's what we all chose.

Joy and I couldn't help but wonder how Bob had "worked on the Other Side to accomplish what's happening now?" Did he keep the detective up at night worrying that Bruce might some day be paroled? Did he plant the idea in the detective's mind of writing the fraudulent letter to the parole board to prevent Bruce's possible release?

Joy shared her excitement about these new developments in Bruce's case at the very next *Sunday of Joy.* Here are her notes from which she spoke.

Like a lotus which grows in the mud, a murder is at the core of our love story... The gruesome murder of Bruce's mother is the seed from which this spiritual document has blossomed.

The murder brought Bob and I together.

The murder made Bob desperate to seek answers beyond the conventional and to attempt to contact his deceased wife on the Other Side. And Bob's desperation to seek answers propelled him beyond his conventional beliefs about reality...and miraculously awakened his connection to his guides and other dimensions of existence.

As his guide whom he called the Director explained, "When you sought to reach your late wife, a rare jump occurred in your abilty to communicate. In almost an instant, you became a conduit to the Universal Spirits...."

In hindsight it's clear that everyone's love was tested. Bob's love for Bruce without knowing for certain

whether he was guilty or not. My love for Bob in sticking with him through all the trips to prison and his health problems that were exacerbated by his heartbreak. And my love for Bruce still not knowing the truth.

Dorka's love was tested, too. Had she said Bruce was innocent and he'd not gone to prison, she would have been handing him a death sentence because his drug use was definitely heading in that direction.

And Bruce's love? He kept the faith and didn't become embittered, but held onto the dream of his eventual freedom.

Inspired by the *Times* article, Joy posted this note on her website to explain why she'd changed the names in her book.

Prior to publishing my book, I changed my name from Joy Lisker to Joy Mitchell to protect my stepson, Bruce Lisker, who is serving a life sentence for a murder he did not commit. Contrary to popular belief, prisoners usually don't know what crime the other inmates have committed. Since matricide is considered one of the worst, Bruce was concerned that my book might endanger him.

For this reason, I changed the names in my book. Bob Lisker became *Bob Mitchell*. Dorka Lisker became *Doris Mitchell*. And Bruce Lisker became *Scott Mitchell*.

On May 22, 2005 Bruce Lisker's story appeared in an explosive article on the front page of the Sunday *Los Angeles Times*. Therefore, I now feel free to divulge the true identities of the individuals in my book.

As Bruce's step-mother, I am very excited about this article because I believe it will reopen his case and will serve as the first step in his 22 year dream of freedom. He's always maintained his innocence and this article goes a long way to proving it.

Joy was now certain that Bruce would regain his freedom. But she wasn't certain she'd live long enough to fulfill her promise to Bob to be there for Bruce when he finally got out of prison. She'd been Bruce's spiritual "mother" for over twenty years and she wanted more than anything to help him readjust to freedom and mother him back to life.

As it turned out, there were many hearings and even more delays, but the wheels of justice ground slowly but surely towards the day of Bruce's freedom. We visited him less frequently now that Joy couldn't see. At a major hearing in late 2005, Bruce was brought before a judge. For a week he sat shackled next to his lawyers in the courtroom. Though Joy and I were no more than 15 feet away, she couldn't see his face. And he wasn't permitted to come over to hug her. That was the last time Joy "saw" Bruce.

· · · · · ·

The day after Valentine's Day 2007, Joy learned that she was "terminal." The cancer had spread to her liver. The next morning Bob reassured her that "dying can be a great adventure."

"Another fucking adventure," she sighed.

After informing her son and daughter and closest friends about her condition, she dictated an email whose subject line read "My Last Adventure."

Dear Friends,

As most of you know I've been dealing with cancer for the past 6 years. Now I seem to be entering the last chapter of my life. On Feb. 15th I learned that the cancer has spread to my liver and that the loss of energy I'd been experiencing for the past few months is the result.

From the very beginning I've chosen quality of life over quantity. And I am still making that choice. Chemo would only make me weaker and doesn't promise a cure. Since I am now 79, I feel that I've had a full and fabulous life. And I'm not afraid to die.

As an astrologer the timing of my transition was not a surprise to me. Also from my experiences talking to my Guides and dozens of souls on the Other Side, I'm not fearful, angry, defeated or depressed. After meeting with my doctor last month I experienced a great deal of sadness for the rest of the day and evening as I thought about everything I would be missing in the future. However, the next morning I awoke with an entirely different perspective.

My Guides assured me that "dying can be a great adventure"—and that's exactly what I intend to make it. So I am choosing to turn this last chapter into one of the best of my life.

I intend to use my limited energy in positive ways rather than in fighting and resisting my condition by focusing my attention on trying to find miraculous cures and alternative healing possibilities. Of course I am open to "miracles" and feel they are more possible when I am vibrating joy, love, gratitude and acceptance rather than all the negative vibrations that come from fear and resistance. And that's where I'm coming from. I'm not TRYING to come from there, that's where I live...that's where I've always lived. Nothing has changed.

I've been a teacher most of my life and I view these last few years with cancer and blindness as a test to see if I could "walk my talk" in spite of these physical challenges. I've received enormous "gifts" from them which proves once again that EVERYTHING that happens is for our benefit.

Every teacher learns a great deal from their students and I'd like to thank you for all you've taught me. But I will continue learning throughout this last adventure. And beyond. As Yogananda stated— "Death is only an experience through which you are meant to learn a great lesson: you cannot die."

With My Love & Blessings,

Joy

Initially, we thought we had anywhere from 6 months to a year, but it turned out to be only seven weeks. With diminishing energy but indomitable spirit, Joy spent the time basking in the love of her family and friends, regaling and thereby reliving stories from her life, and designing her "graduation party." Besides choosing music, centerpieces and menus for the 200+ guests, she wrote the following meditation for the event. Even after she was gone she would still be teaching joy.

Cancer gave me many gifts. Blindness gave me many more gifts. Every experience is for our highest good. Keeping this in mind, reflect now on your own painful experiences in the past and ask to be shown the Gift. The certainty that EVERYTHING is ultimately for our benefit, and that THAT IS THE PERFECTION IN LIFE has been the secret to my happiness. And I hope you will make it your own.

Two days before her transition, Joy wrote a poem she wanted read at her party in which she offered to be a "spirit guide" like Bob had been for her.

"Opening to Joy"

I have not left you,
I did not die.
I will speak to you in the sacred silences
Of your days and nights.

Listen for my voice
And trust what you hear.
Ask your questions and I will tell you the Truth.

I look forward to sharing
All the wisdom I will be learning
From the Other Side.
So open to joy and let it fill
Every moment of your life.

Surrounded by her children and closest friends, I held Joy as she breathed her last breath and left her body at noon on Good Friday, April 6th, 2007.

Her party was a magnificent *Celebration of Life* just as she planned. Her children performed her favorite music. From prison Bruce sent the following eulogy for his step-mother.

Joy's transition last Friday was elegant and dignified. Given the impeccable way she lived her life, that didn't surprise me. She avoided great pain in her final days, and is now soaring high above us all, unconstrained by earthly bonds, visiting us at will!

Yet I'm still not happy about it. That was no "Good" Friday.

It is ironic that our dearest ones seem to leave us at the very moment when we've never loved them more, and that usually it's the one we've lost whom we wish could comfort us the most.

Silver linings are great—and ultimately true—but some of our hearts have been broken into a thousand tiny shards by this, and it will take a lifetime to truly heal. Joy was always there to help me discover my authentic self on a matter when I frequently sought her guidance. She knew me so well it often surprised me. In her heart, and in mine, I was one of her natural-born kids. And mother me she did. Her gentle encouragement and understanding over time cultivated within me a confidence I had always lacked. When my father died 12 years ago, I never thought I could love—or miss—

another human being as much as I did him. I was wrong. She'd become my mom, and my world would never be the same.

Her echo will resonate in my heart throughout eternity. Thank God.

It's been said that at the end of our lives, after all our successes and failures, the value of our time on earth will be measured by how much we have loved.

How awesome! Joy loved so many, so much! That's why she was and will always be a Great One. Her love was a splendid magic that brought all of us to the daily threshold of jubilant expectation whereby we entered into a willingness to accept the totality of human experience with equal parts reverence and bliss.

> *"Wisdom is knowing we are all One.*
> *'Love' is what it feels like.*
> *'Compassion' is what it acts like."*
> *(Author Unkown)*

There is peace in knowing we are all One in celebrating the life of a miraculous soul who until days ago walked among us, who felt like love, and who was the embodiment of compassion.

May the peace with which Joy lived her own life remain with us all until we rejoin her for the next leg of our grand journey.

Bruce Lisker

I spoke last and wasn't sure I'd be able to give a eulogy, but desperately wanted to tell the world about an amazing being called Joy and the wonderful love we shared. I began with these words....

I know it's not usual for the grieving spouse to speak at the memorial service. But I have to speak today, I have the rest of my life to cry. I've been the luckiest man in the world. Right now, and for the time being, I'm the saddest....

Buoyed by Joy's love, I managed to speak for nearly half an hour.

And then came the darkness...

· · · · · ·

In the depths of my grief an extraordinary thing happened— Joy began communicating with *me* from the Other Side. She guided me on an incredible journey to heal my grief. She became *my* "spirit guide." Ultimately, like the final scene in the movie "Ghost," Joy found someone—a willing medium—through whom she literally *loved me back to life.*

Needing to chronicle my miraculous experience and hoping it would inspire others going through grief, I wrote a memoir entitled, ***JOYride: How My Late Wife Loved Me Back To Life.*** My experience of Joy "beyond the veil" was so extraordinary I addressed it in the very first lines of the Introduction.

Like all great love stories ours is about sex and death. The alpha and omega. Beginning and End. It's also about the eternal nature of love.

Many people will be shocked by our story; others may be inspired. Some will find it ridiculous; others miraculous. Of course, there will be those who consider it blasphemous. Most, however, will find it hard to believe. I can't blame them. If I hadn't experienced it myself I wouldn't have believed it either. But this is a true story.

It happened to me. I call it *JOYride*.

As I worked on *JOYride*, I recalled Joy writing in the Epilogue of *Love Ever After* that she'd discovered from Bob that there was a greater purpose to our relationship, and that was "shining a new light on two of the most misunderstood areas of our lives—sex and death." At the time, Joy was referring to my unfinished novel, *The Secret Sex Life of Angels*.* To my astonishment, I realized that *JOYride* was the fulfillment of that purpose.

· · · · · ·

A few weeks after completing *JOYride*, a federal judge overturned Bruce's murder conviction and, to the accompaniment of TV cameras and frontpage headlines, he was released from prison after serving 26 years for a crime he did not commit.

On the morning of August 13th, 2009, the Eyewitness Newscast's graphic flashed, "Lisker Freed!" while the TV anchor announced, "Last week a judge overturned Bruce Lisker's conviction because of false evidence and sloppy defense work. Lisker walked out of Mule Creek State Prison this morning."

In an impromptu press conference in a park near the prison Bruce spoke to the media in a voice flooded with

The Secret Sex Life of Angels was published in September 2016.

emotion. "It's a joyous day—the best day of my life!" Climbing into the pickup truck that would drive him back to Los Angeles, a reporter asked, "What are you going to do first when you get back to LA?" Bruce thought for a moment, then with a wistful smile replied, "Take a swim."

Eight hours later I sat poolside on a hot August afternoon watching a man who'd been caged for over a quarter of a century take his first swim. And I wept. For Bruce. For Joy. For Bob. For justice. I was overcome with an indescribable happiness that I like to think was partly due to Bob and Joy celebrating in the Afterlife.

At the age of 44, Bruce came "home" to live with me where he would experience his first taste of freedom and take his first tentative steps towards rebuilding the life he lost. Joy couldn't be there to witness this nearly miraculous righting of a terrible wrong, but I was. And it was a great honor.

With Bruce free and living with me, I began to see his story in a larger context and Joy's image of "a lotus growing out of the mud" came back to me. Out of the mud of this family tragedy—in which a mother was brutally murdered and her teenage son wrongfully convicted of the crime—has grown the lotus of these inspirational messages of life-after-death and eternal love.

Bob's torment about losing his wife *and* his son—a tragedy of almost biblical proportions—drove this conservative lawyer, ex-marine and pillar of the community to attempt to contact the spirit of his dead wife to find out who killed her, setting the stage for the afterlife communications Joy wrote about in this book.

As I helped Bruce adjust to his new found freedom— using an ATM card, filling a tank of gas, obtaining a driver's license—it began to dawn on me all the ways I was connected to his story, especially now that I was standing in Bob's role of "father."

Bob gave Joy the 12 Step program to attract a new love — *me*. I was the "home" Bruce came to after his release from prison. In this context, **JOYride** was also a part of the larger story — which I'd begun to think of as *The Joyful Redemption* — that began with the murder and Bruce's wrongful conviction 26 years ago and ended with his release.

Incredibly, out of a pool of blood, brutality and a blatant miscarriage of justice have blossomed not one, but *two* first hand accounts of life-after-death communication. In this "afterlife saga" both Bruce's father and step-mother became "spirit guides." It's wild! It's crazy! And yet it's true! In fact, the odds that Bruce would ever regain his freedom were just as improbable. And miraculous.

The Lord works in mysterious ways.... Why this murder and family tragedy generated these two testaments to life-after-death is a mystery. And what greater purpose there might be to the unfolding of Bruce Lisker's life, only time will tell.

— *I. J. Weinstock*, Los Angeles 2010
joyousone@aol.com

P.S. *The Secret Sex Life of Angels,* was published in September 2016.

℘ *Acknowledgements* ℃

First, last and always, I want to thank my late husband, Bob, for providing the wisdom and information contained in this book.

But this book would not exist at all without two people who became the wind beneath my wings—my beautiful daughter, Terri, and my incredible partner, Jerry. It was my daughter who first suggested turning my conversations with Bob into a book and helped give birth to this labor of love. Thank you, Terri, for motivating me with your love and enthusiasm, for your unflagging belief in me, and for being my number one critic, cheerleader and nudge.

Even after its birth, this book might never have been completed without Jerry's constant encouragement and insightful guidance. His tender loving care every step of the way gave me the courage and the impetus to share this material with the world. Thank you from the bottom of my heart for being there every time I asked for help, for putting aside your own projects to assist me, and for sharing in this journey to a depth beyond all measure or expectation.

My deepest gratitude and appreciation also goes to those who have so generously gifted me with their perceptive comments and enthusiastic support: first, to my extraordinary son, Elliot, whose love, loyalty and stamp of approval means so much to me; to my daughter-in-law, Kate, an accomplished writer who so generously offered the wisdom of her experience; Suzanne Biddle, my dear friend since the third grade who gave me the book title; Jackie Cole, my soul sister from many lifetimes; and Marge Engesser for the awesome cover design.

Heartfelt thanks to my incomparable cheering section: Gael and Paul Kennedy, Eileen Factor, Harriet Gibson, Margie Nunan, Susan Nanus, Lorraine Marshall, Bryan Simon, Joy and Bruce Webster, Norma Herron, Beanie Polsky, Brina Rickerman, Elaine Rupprecht, Doralee Jacobson, Yvonne Hyatt, Shakti Copeland, Nellie Reyes, Christiana Carter, Kevin Larson, Philip di Franco and Lanny Gooding.

ᔆᴐ *About the Author* ᥣᐧ

As a professional astrologer, writer, teacher, hypnotherapist and minister, Joy Mitchell Lisker spent over 50 years helping others find their own path of joy.

After a decade of reading horoscopes for thousands of clients (including many Hollywood stars), teaching and lecturing to schools, charities and civic organizations in Los Angeles, Joy became the resident astrologer on two local TV shows and appeared as a guest on numerous others.

In 1976 Joy wrote, produced and hosted the first television series on astrology in America, which debuted in Los Angeles and aired in more than a dozen cities throughout California. Subsequently, she held the position of vice-president and chief astrologer of XII Signs, publishers of the monthly *Starscrolls* found in supermarkets and vending machines around the world.

Joy's first book was entitled **Days and Nights For Making Love: Sexual Timing with Astrology** (1980).

After Bob Lisker's death in 1995, Joy communicated with him almost daily for two years. In 2000, she published these channeled conversations in a memoir entitled, *LOVE EVER AFTER: How My Husband Became My Spirit Guide*.

In 1997, Joy met and fell in love with Jerry Weinstock. Though he was nineteen years younger, they spent the next ten years blissfully happy. *Sexy at Seventy*—an article Joy wrote about her sex life—was published in, *Our Turn, Our Time*, a collection of essays by women over fifty about what they find most fulfilling in the second half of their lives. Joy wanted to let women know that it's never too late for a great sex life and that it can even get better with age!

In 2001, Joy was diagnosed with breast cancer, yet despite this health challenge she and Jerry created the *"12 Steps to Finding Your Soulmate"* workshop based on the 12 step program to manifest one's dreams Bob had given her from the Afterlife.

When Joy became "legally blind" due to macular degeneration, she gained her psychic vision and for several years at monthly gatherings called a *Sunday of Joy* she answered people's most pressing questions about their lives.

Joy succumbed to cancer on Good Friday 2007. She is survived by her husband, Jerry Weinstock, her children—the singer Terri Nunn and composer Elliot Anders—and her stepson, Bruce Lisker.

Find out more at www.IJWeinstock.com

Available on
Amazon
http://amzn.to/2j529sl

CreateSpace
http://bit.ly/2jVpb60

JOYride
How My Late Wife Loved Me Back To Life

by I. J. Weinstock

Joy and Jerry were soulmates, in fact, they were literally a "match-made-in heaven" according to Joy's channeled memoir, **Love Ever After**.

When Jerry lost Joy to breast cancer, he was devastated. Then a remarkable thing happened—Joy began communicating with him from the Afterlife and led him on an incredible journey to heal his grief. Ultimately, like the final scene in the movie, *Ghost*, Joy found someone, a willing medium, through whom she literally loved him back to life.

"Most people will be shocked by our story. I can't blame them. I'd heard of life-after-death, but sex-after-death? If I hadn't experienced it myself, I wouldn't have believed it either. But this is a true story. It happened to me." ~ I. J. Weinstock, from the Introduction

JOYride is as fantastic a love story as the hit movie, *Ghost*, except it's REAL! This book will change the way you view life, death, love and what is possible.

FINALIST in the 2012 USA Best Book Awards

Find out more at www.IJWeinstock.com

Available on
Amazon
http://amzn.to/2j59h8c

CreateSpace
http://bit.ly/2jHoks8

LOVE MAY BE THE ANSWER
BUT LOSS POSES THE QUESTIONS

In the agony and inconsolable grief of losing a loved one,
we find ourselves asking questions we've never asked before...

When we say we've "lost" our loved one, the truth is we're lost.
The world as we've known it no longer exists. The right questions
are like a trail in the wilderness that can lead us out of the darkness
toward the light of a new life that is forever changed.

THE QUESTIONS DETERMINE THE QUEST

Grief Quest utilizes a unique question-based L.O .V.E. Process—

> **L** — Love your memories
>
> **O** — Open to your grief
>
> **V** — Value the gifts
>
> **E** — Embrace your life

The questions in *Grief Quest* will help you memorialize your
loved one. The simple act of recording your memories
is a tribute to the love and life you shared.

If you embark on this *Grief Quest* you'll get to know yourself
and your relationship with your loved one on a deeper level
than you thought possible.

I. J. Weinstock created *Grief Quest* out of his extraordinary
experience of love and loss. His award-winning memoir, *JOYride:
How My Late Wife Loved Me Back To Life*, tells the remarkable story
of how the spirit of his late wife, Joy, gave him *Keys to Healing Loss*
and led him on an incredible journey that healed his grief. He leads
workshops at international conferences on grief, and counsels the
bereaved as a *grief guide*.

My Year Exploring Love
&
Discovering A Secret To Happiness

the *Love Spell* experiment

I. J. WEINSTOCK

Find out more at www.IJWeinstock.com

Available on
Amazon
http://amzn.to/2ixxnfL

CreateSpace
http://bit.ly/2jVvbeY

The LoveSpell Experiment

by I. J. Weinstock

What Do You Love?

This simple yet profound question
inspired an extraordinary exploration
into the very nature of Love.

While celebrating New Year's Eve, I. J. Weinstock heard his late
wife, Joy, ask him that simple question—*What do you love?*

His answer became a year-long quest in which
he learned more than 1001 things about love
and discovered a secret to happiness.

The LoveSpell Experiment
is a uniquely intimate document that reveals
a key to unlock the treasure chest of one's life!

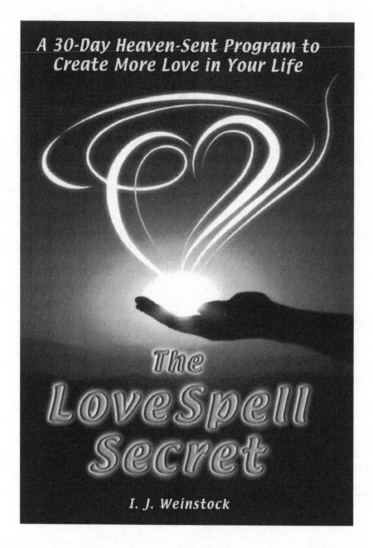

Find out more at www.IJWeinstock.com

Available on
Amazon
http://amzn.to/2hQNUGx

CreateSpace
http://bit.ly/2kb1k5O

The LoveSpell Secret

A 30-Day Heaven-Sent Program
to Create More Love in Your Life

Inspired by his *LoveSpell Experiment,* I. J. Weinstock has created a workbook, The LoveSpell Secret: *A 30-Day Heaven-Sent Program to Create More Love in Your Life,* to help you develop the habit of asking and answering one of life's most important questions—*What do you love?*

To actually grow the love in your life, you can't just read about it, you have to do it. If you do it for the next 30 days— *Acknowledge, Appreciate* and pay *Attention* to the love in your life—you'll develop the habit of looking at your life through love-colored glasses, receive the amazing benefits of your in-creased dose of *Vitamin L,* and discover that the power to grow the love in your life is in your heart and in your hands.

"What do you love?" What a profound and necessary question.
Thanks for reminding us to ask the question
on a regular basis. To paraphrase the wisdom in this
handbook, I think we'd all do well to acknowledge,
appreciate and pay attention to this guide!

— *Dr. Seth Kadish*
"Pop Your Patterns: The No-Nonsense Way
to Change Your Life"

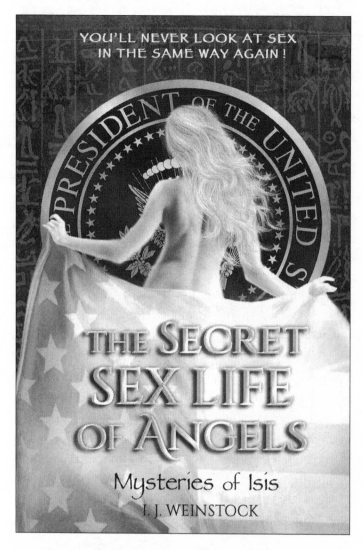

The Secret Sex Life of Angels
by I. J Weinstock

In a world with no future, one man is offered a secret key from the past to unlock the greatest mystery of all.

On the 100th day of his presidency, Adam Hart discovers that to fulfill his oath of office he must embark on a sexual odyssey that could determine the fate of the world.

The Secret Sex Life of Angels combines the intrigue and controversy of *The Da Vinci Code* with the spirituality and eroticism of the *Kama Sutra* in a fantastic saga about the sacred nature of sex.

"Every man needs to read *The Secret Sex Life of Angels.* Every woman needs to have her man read this book."

"You'll never think about sex in the same way again!"

"This is the book everyone will be talking about."

Made in the USA
Columbia, SC
14 September 2017